IN HIS P

The Alternative Service Book

A prayer book and guide to
Confirmation, Communion
and Church Teaching

by

DENIS E. TAYLOR

lately Dean of Brisbane

RELIGIOUS AND MORAL EDUCATION PRESS
An Imprint of Arnold-Wheaton

Printed in Great Britain by
A. Wheaton & Co. Ltd, Exeter

ISBN 0 08-031756-1 flexi
ISBN 0 08-031757-X hard

FOREWORD

By the former Bishop of St Andrews

A BOOK is like a child. After it is conceived in its author's mind it remains hidden and secret while it slowly takes shape, but on its appearance in the world it assumes an independent life of its own, its begetter looking on with wistful hope, trusting that it may find a welcome and have a prosperous life.

Next to the privilege of being a father is the honour of being a godfather; and I am proud to stand sponsor for this little book which is now in your hands. Without doubt it will keep the 'promises' which are involved in its appearance. It is on the greatest of all subjects, on which our immortal well-being depends, and will teach its readers (old as well as young) how to 'draw near'.

Perhaps the highest praise I can give to it is to say that it is a characteristic product of its author, and he is well qualified to write it. As he grows older (like Wordsworth's 'Happy Warrior') he keeps undimmed in his mind the experience of youth; and now, with the wisdom of the mature, can speak with understanding to the heart of the young.

LUMSDEN BARKWAY

ACKNOWLEDGEMENTS

CONTENTS

                                                            Page
Prayer—Morning Prayers—The Parts of Prayer   7
—Evening Prayers—Daily Intercessions—Acts
of Adoration—Praying Every Day—A Scheme
of Intercession and Prayer Notebook

What Is the Church?—Confirmation—The   27
Duties of a Churchman—Archbishops' Guide
to Duties of Church Membership—The
Church's Books: the Bible, the Prayer Book,
The Alternative Service Book 1980—The
Church's Year—The Church's Clothes

What Is the Holy Communion?—How Often   52
Shall I Make My Communion?—Our Preparation
for Holy Communion—During the Eucharist

How We Are Forgiven—Overhauling Ourselves   62
—Questions for Self-examination—Confessing
Our Sins

THE HOLY COMMUNION
according to Rite A, The Alternative Service   71
Book 1980

IN HIS PRESENCE

PART I: PRAYER

EACH NEW DAY

'I am with you alway.'

At the beginning of a new day our aim is to offer to God all that lies ahead and to ask for his help and for the knowledge that he is with us, present beside us all the time. For he *is* always with us, though we, busy with the day's work and cares, may often forget him.

On the morning before the battle of Edgehill, the Cavalier Sir Jacob Astley prayed:

> Lord, I shall be very busy this day.
> If I forget thee,
> Do not thou forget me.

At the start of the new day, then let us offer it to our Father, praying above all that we may have a clear sense of his presence.

> Closer is he than breathing and
> nearer than hands and feet.

Kneel. Remember that our Lord is very near. Say reverently and thoughtfully:

In the name of the Father, and of the Son, and of the Holy Spirit.

Thank God for the rest and safety of the night now past, for health and powers renewed. Offer to God the day that is beginning:

Blessed Lord, I thank you for rest and safety
   through the hours of night.
For this new day in which to serve you,
For powers of mind and body made new once more,
I worship and adore your glorious name.

Praise and adore God, using these verses from the Te Deum:

You are God and we praise you:
   you are the Lord and we acclaim you;
you are the eternal Father:
   all creation worships you.
To you all angels, all the powers of heaven:
   cherubim and seraphim sing in endless praise,
Holy holy holy Lord, God of power and might:
   heaven and earth are full of your glory.
Throughout the world the holy Church acclaims you:
   Father of majesty unbounded;
your true and only Son, worthy of all worship:
   and the Holy Spirit, advocate and guide.
You, Christ, are the King of glory:
   the eternal Son of the Father.

PRAYERS

Day by day we bless you:
　we praise your name for ever.
Keep us today, Lord, from all sin:
　have mercy on us, Lord, have mercy.
Lord, show us your love and mercy:
　for we put our trust in you.
In you, Lord, is our hope:
　let us not be confounded at the end.

Ask for help in the coming day:

Most Holy Jesus, Friend and Master, you are ever near; keep me today from sin in all I think and do and say.

Help me to know that you are by my side to give me strength when I am tempted, and wisdom when I am puzzled or in doubt.

Blessed Lord, I offer this day to you. May everything that I do be to your glory and reflect your love. Help me to know that in doing my work I am doing your will, and that in serving others, I am serving you.

In this way, may I grow closer to you, my Master and my Friend.

Try to be up in time to do some of your work of Intercession. Turn to pages 20 to 26 for this.

Our Father ... Amen.

May the Grace of our Lord Jesus Christ, and the Love of God, and the fellowship of the Holy Spirit, be with me in all I do this day and for evermore. Amen.

THE PARTS OF PRAYER

Each night our private prayers should be modelled like this:

ADORATION First, love, adore and praise God in whom we live and move, and have our being. Praise him for his noble acts, praise him for his excellent greatness. Adore him for Jesus Christ. Love him because he first loved us and gave himself for us.

CONFESSION A sense of all that God is and all he does for us at once brings home our own unworthiness, how often we fail to live up even to our own ideals, how poor our fight against temptation, how weak our efforts to pray better, how uncostly our work for others and for our Lord. So we confess these our sins to God, and ask forgiveness.

THANKSGIVING The knowledge that when we are truly sorry and really mean to do better, we are forgiven makes thankfulness well up in our hearts, and we set ourselves to remember our many blessings—health, home, food, work, friends, play, our Church, all the joy of being alive—and we return thanks to God our Father.

SUPPLICATION Having adored God, having confessed our sinfulness, having thanked him for all his goodness and loving-kindness, then and then only we ask for more blessings. We make our supplications first for the needs of others, for great causes, for friends and for enemies. These are our Intercessions. Afterwards we pray for ourselves—we tell God our hopes, our joys, our fears, our desires, our needs. These are our Petitions.

Such prayers are A-C-T-S indeed,

true ACTS of worship.

Kneel. Remember that our Lord is very near. Say reverently and thoughtfully:

In the name of the Father, and of the Son, and of the Holy Spirit.

Be very still. Let the rush and hurry of the day die away as you kneel in silence in his presence. Think of the wonder and majesty of God the Creator of this universe, of earth and sea, of stars and illimitable space. Try to express your wonder and love.

Adoration

Blessed are you, Lord God, from of old and for ever. Yours, Lord, is the greatness, the power, the glory, the splendour and the majesty; for everything in heaven and on earth is yours; yours is the sovereignty and you are exalted over all as head. Wealth and honour come from you; you rule over all ... And now, we give you thanks, our God, and praise your glorious name.

I will bless the Lord continually:
  his praise shall be always in my mouth.

Jesu, my Lord, I thee adore.
O make me love thee more and more.

(Often use other words of adoration. Some are given on page 16.)

PRAYERS

Confession

Think back over the day. What good have you left undone? Have you said or done anything wrong or mean? Sometimes use the questions for self-examination on page 65. Always do this before Communion. When you have thought back carefully over the day, tell God where you have failed.

Almighty God, our heavenly Father, I have sinned against you and against my fellow men, in thought and word and deed, through negligence, through weakness, through my own deliberate fault. Especially I have failed in these ways ... I am truly sorry and repent of all my sins. For the sake of your Son Jesus Christ, who died for us, forgive me all that is past; and grant that I may serve you in newness of life; to the glory of your name. Amen.

Sometimes you may like to express special penitence in the solemn words of Psalm 51.

Have mercy on me, O God, in your enduring goodness:
according to the fullness of your compassion blot out my offences.
Wash me thoroughly from my wickedness:
and cleanse me from my sin.
For I acknowledge my rebellion:
and my sin is ever before me.
Create in me a clean heart, O God:
and renew a right spirit within me.

Pray earnestly in your own words for forgiveness.

Thanksgiving

Not only does God forgive our sins when we repent, and for this we should thank him gladly, but our life is full of blessings. Health, home, food, friends are only a few, and there is the greatest blessing of all—the friendship of our Lord Jesus Christ. These suggestions may remind you of blessings for which to thank God:

Health	Work	Clothing
Parents	Home	Food
My Church	Friends, especially	
Good times, especially	Beauty in God's handiwork, e.g. country, garden, sea	
Help in temptation, especially	Beauty in man's handiwork, e.g. music, painting, books	

When you have considered, then thank God with all your heart:

Almighty and everlasting God, I praise and thank you for all your countless goodness and mercies towards me. Especially I thank you for ... Help me to be truly thankful for these and for all your good gifts by giving myself to your service and by waiting before you in holiness and righteousness all my days; through Jesus Christ our Lord, to whom with you and the Holy Spirit be all honour and glory, for ever and ever. Amen.

PRAYERS

Supplication

*There are, of course, some special people and needs
you will wish to pray for every night:*

Father .... Mother ....

Husband or Wife ....

Home, special difficulties .... needs ....

Brothers .... Sisters ....

Special friends ....

Relations ....

Anyone seriously ill or dying ....

One who has died ....

My own needs and hopes ....

*Turn to your Intercession Notes for each day of the
week, pages 20 to 26.*

*Sum up your Adoration, Confession, Thanksgiving
and Supplication in our Lord's own words:*

Our Father...

**Into your hands, O Lord, I commend myself and all
for whom I have prayed tonight. Keep us in your
loving care and bless us all, I pray. Amen.**

ACTS OF ADORATION

'O praise ye the Lord.'

Here are some glorious words with which to offer God your praise.

Holy, holy, holy Lord, God of power and might, heaven and earth are full of your glory. Hosanna in the highest.

Glory to the Father and to the Son and to the Holy Spirit; as it was in the beginning, is now, and shall be for ever. Amen.

Bless the Lord, the God of our fathers:
   sing his praise and exalt him for ever.
Bless his holy and glorious name:
   sing his praise and exalt him for ever.
Bless him in his holy and glorious temple:
   sing his praise and exalt him for ever.
Bless him on the throne of his kingdom:
   sing his praise and exalt him for ever.
Bless him in the heights of heaven:
   sing his praise and exalt him for ever.
Bless the Father, the Son and the Holy Spirit:
   sing his praise and exalt him for ever.

Now to him who is able to do immeasurably more than all we can ask or conceive, by the power which is at work among us, to him be glory in the Church and in Christ Jesus throughout all ages. Amen.

O Lord our Governor:
   how glorious is your name in all the earth!
When I consider your heavens, the work of your
   fingers:
   the moon and the stars which you have set in order,
what is man, that you should be mindful of him:
   or the son of man that you should care for him?
Yet you have made him little less than a god:
   and have crowned him with glory and honour.
O Lord our Governor:
   how glorious is your name in all the earth.

Psalm 8

Bless the Lord, O my soul:
   O Lord my God, how great you are!
Clothed with majesty and honour:
   wrapped in light as in a garment.
I will sing to the Lord as long as I live:
   I will praise my God while I have any being.
May my meditation be pleasing to him:
   for my joy shall be in the Lord.

Psalm 104

Our hymn-books contain many magnificent acts of praise. Use these sometimes in your private prayers, e.g.

Holy, holy, holy, Lord God Almighty

and

My God, how wonderful thou art.

A SCHEME OF INTERCESSION

To pray for others, that is, to intercede, is a most important work. It is real work, hard work, service of the highest order.

If we pray only for ourselves and, maybe, our little circle, our prayers are *really* selfish. How tired we get of folk who can talk only about themselves! We do not want God to feel like that about us.

There is service and adventure in learning to take your part in the prayer work of the Church. You will find it makes your prayers more interesting and satisfying. You *know* you have done something useful and important.

But it is not easy. There are many difficulties, such as wandering thoughts, and your own weariness at bedtime. Why not make it your habit to drop in to your church for ten minutes on your way home from work every day to do this other work? If you do not pass near enough for that, could you not make your prayer time immediately after your meal, before going out for the evening?

Above all perseverance is needed. The Devil will try hard to break down any good habit you build up—he will put many difficulties in the way.

Remember that Jesus told us to go on praying and not grow weary of trying. He reminded us that perseverance in prayer is rewarded when he told of the widow who cried to an unjust judge for justice day after day, until the man at last granted her request because he was so thoroughly sick of her! Imagine our Lord likening himself to an unjust judge! But there are several stories Jesus told with a twinkle in his eye. One of these was on this subject of persevering in intercession—about the man who needed bread for a belated traveller and went to knock up a neighbour, already in bed, to borrow a loaf. He went on shouting for it till the neighbour just *had* to get up and give it. We are to persevere with our prayers.

Prayer is work. Work needs method.

On the next pages there is a scheme for Intercession arranged over the days of the week. Without an ordered scheme you are bound to forget much for which you should be praying. Hence this scheme for each day of the week and space to add your own notes.

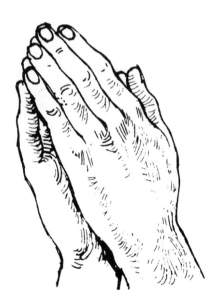

A PRAYER NOTEBOOK

SUNDAY—The Church of God

Sunday is the weekly commemoration of the rising of Christ from the tomb, to live and reign for evermore. The Church carries on his work.

Pray for

Your Bishop(s).   Your own parish clergy.

Members of your congregation, especially ....
....

Church workers—choir, Sunday-school teachers, sidesmen, servers, wardens, vestry, ladies' guild members, etc., especially ....

More priests. Remember the need for more manpower at home and overseas. For any thinking of ordination ....

The world-wide Church. Any need (e.g., unity, greater faith, converting the indifferent) ....
....

Any approaching great world event affecting the whole Church ....

That Christians may learn to give generously of their money and time in God's service.

That priests and lay people may strive to bring those outside who never worship into membership.

MONDAY—The Church Overseas

Pause to remember that but for the missionary zeal of the Apostles and early Christians we should have been left in paganism and fear. A first duty of a Christian is to win others to Christ. Thank God for the heroism of missionaries and that in most lands today there is a strong indigenous Church.

Pray for

Any missionary you know personally ....

Mission priests, doctors, nurses, teachers, agriculturalists, carpenters and mechanics, especially ....

The people among whom they work ... that they may have faith and courage to overcome opposition of family or neighbours in accepting Christ.

Indigenous priests, catechists, teachers, that they may give a fine witness among their own people.

The missionary societies' home headquarters.

Removal of colour barriers so that racial segregation and hatred may be overcome.

Churchpeople to understand still better and care more for the world mission of the Church.

(If you know little about the great work overseas ask the clergy for the monthly papers published by all missionary societies.)

TUESDAY—The Nations

Think of the events which are in the news, international problems, racial difficulties, peoples striving for independence, etc., etc. Bring to God the happenings which seem to you most urgent or dangerous and pray that God's will may be done.

Pray for

The United Nations, that it may build true fellowship between the nations.

The hungry in many lands.

Our own statesmen, especially ....

Leaders of other lands, especially ....

The people in lands without political freedom ......
....

Any who lead in the struggle for freedom ....

Christians persecuted for their religion or politics, or in fear or want, especially ....

Clubs and Fellowships

Pray for

Any club, association or fellowship, youth or adult, to which you belong—sporting, trade unionist, political, cultural or religious.

Members, especially ....

Chaplain ....

Particular needs or problems ....

22

WEDNESDAY—**Earners and Industry**

Pray for

Your office, shop or factory friends ....

The head, and others in authority ....

Those working in difficult, dangerous, or unhealthy conditions.

(If you do not know any personally, pray for miners, seamen, iron workers at blast furnaces, etc., those on night shift.)

Any unemployed or in money difficulties ....

Any unhappy in their jobs ....

Anyone unpopular ....

Difficulties at work ....

Schools, Colleges and Universities

Pray for

Your school, college or university ....

Your friends, especially ....

Teachers, lecturers, that they may inspire a love of the Christian faith, and appreciation of beauty, truth and real goodness ....

All keen young Churchpeople to see in teaching a great field of service for Christ ....

Any thinking of teaching, especially ....

THURSDAY—The Lonely and Old

Thursday is the day of Christ's lonely temptation in the Garden of Gethsemane.

Pray for

The lonely, particularly old people who have no one to care for and love them, especially ....
....

Thursday was also the day of Christ's Ascension to Heaven.

Thank God for the triumph of Jesus.

The Nation and Commonwealth

Pray for

Any part of the Commonwealth you know ....

Any Commonwealth problem (e.g., racial unity, political independence) ....

The Sovereign and Royal Family ....

The Prime Minister ....

Any M.P., local councillor, or magistrate, especially
....

Urgent local or national questions (e.g., housing, crime, etc.) ....

All the nations of the Commonwealth to be a power for peace throughout the world.

FRIDAY—**All Who Need Christ's Love**

Friday is the day of the Crucifixion of Jesus.

Pray for

A clearer realization of God's great love for us—love so great that he was willing to die for us.

Greater willingness to work for God.

Unbelievers—any you know who seldom or never worship God, especially ....

(Perhaps someone in your office or home.)

Children without parents or home or religion, especially ....

Pray for

Doctors and nurses, especially ....

(Think of them in consulting room and hospital. Remember by name any you know.)

Sufferers. Any ill or suffering person you know. Lift them up to our Lord who loves them and suffered for all. Pray for each by name ....

Old people, especially ....
Homes for the aged, especially ....

(If you do not know any orphanages, rescue homes, hostels, or homes for old folk, ask your clergy to get someone along to talk about them. Much good work is little known. Much help is needed.)

Pray for

The Faithful departed, especially ....

SATURDAY—The Church at Home

Pray for

More manpower.

(Think of the inadequacy of one priest to thousands of people. Pray that more men will feel the call to the priesthood. They may not be conscious that God is calling them. Your prayers may help them realize.)

Pray for

More women workers, as missionaries, nurses, teachers, youth leaders, community-centre workers, deaconesses or Sunday-school teachers.

(Pray for any whom you think God might use in these ways. Perhaps he wants you?)

Pray that

Churchpeople may rise to the challenge to bring the Church to new housing areas. For this work in your diocese.

Pray for

Any special project in your own congregation ....
....
Sunday schools ....
Efforts to reach young people who attend no church
....
Any preparing for Confirmation, especially ....
....

(Are you making your Communion tomorrow? Turn to page 57.)

PART II: THE CHURCH

WHAT IS THE CHURCH?

What is the Church? A Society—a divine Society because founded by Jesus Christ. Whitsunday is called the Birthday of the Church.

What is the Church for? To carry on what Jesus began—to teach people the goodness, holiness and love of God and his purpose for men; to restore the relationship between God and man broken by man's disobedience which we call sin. The Church is to be the family of God's people, uniting them in worship and in work to set up his reign of justice and love, and helping them to bear witness to him by the quality of their lives.

How do we become members? Entrance to the Church is by Baptism, in which a person is made a member of Christ, the child of God and an inheritor of the Kingdom of Heaven.

What do members try to do? *Renounce*, that is, have nothing to do with anything evil, mean or second rate; *believe* and be tremendously happy about our Christian faith; *keep* God's holy will and commandments made plain through the Bible, the teaching of the Church, and our conscience; be fellow-workers with Jesus in spreading kindness and joy, setting up the reign of God on earth, his 'kingdom' of goodness and love; join together to worship and adore our Creator, the God 'Who made and loveth all'. Members try by prayer, the Sacraments, self-discipline and service to grow in the knowledge and love of Jesus.

What does the Church do for her members? Calls them together for worship; is the channel whereby God strengthens them for the difficulties and temptations of life by giving them the Holy Spirit in Baptism and Confirmation; refreshes them constantly through the Sacrament of the Body and Blood of Christ.

Teaches them about God, his intentions for men and their eternal destiny; gives them special help at the crossroads of life, e.g., marriage, illness; acts as a channel whereby the repentant receive forgiveness; joins them in a happy fellowship, the Church, an army pledged to carry on the work Christ began.

The Church includes not only her members in this world, the Church Militant here on earth (militant means fighting, i.e., waging war against sin and evil); but also those who have passed on to the life beyond. They are called the Church Expectant (i.e., waiting while being made perfect) and the Church Triumphant in Heaven.

Who are the Church's ministers? The Church has a threefold ministry: bishops, priests and deacons. A man is made deacon first, and may not celebrate Holy Communion, pronounce Absolution nor give the Blessing. After one year as deacon he is ordained priest and can exercise every function of the Ministry except those reserved for bishops (following the example of the Apostles).

Bishops only may administer Confirmation (see Acts 8 quoted below) or ordain a man as deacon or priest. The bishops take the place of the Apostles, deriving their authority from Christ's commission to the Apostles, handed down to them today. This is called the Apostolic Succession. Bishops have oversight of dioceses. These may have as few as a dozen parishes, but in some countries have as many as four or five hundred. Titles vary from country to country, but the bishop of a large diocese may have a suffragan or assistant bishop(s) and also be aided by archdeacons and rural deans who supervise groups of parishes. The dean is the chief minister of the cathedral, but if the cathedral has a parish the title provost is used.

A group of dioceses forms a province under an Archbishop, who may be referred to as the Metropolitan. In Scotland the title Archbishop is avoided and the bishop elected head of the province is called the Primus, meaning 'first among equals'. Where a country has several provinces (e.g. Canada) one of the Archbishops is appointed Primate.

CONFIRMATION

Confirmation is in the Bible. It was practised by the Apostles. We read about it in the New Testament. The Church has administered it ever since.

Confirmation: In the New Testament
From Acts, Chap. 8

Philip came down to a city in Samaria and began proclaiming the Messiah to them ... When they came to believe Philip with his good news about the kingdom of God and the name of Jesus Christ, they were baptized, men and women alike ... The Apostles in Jerusalem now heard that Samaria had accepted the word of God. They sent off Peter and John, who went down there and prayed for the converts, asking that they might receive the Holy Spirit ... So Peter and John laid their hands on them and they received the Holy Spirit.

Confirmation: Receiving the Holy Spirit

Philip had gone to Samaria preaching and teaching. He baptized his converts, just as your priest would. Then the Apostles came from Jerusalem and 'laid their hands on them and they received the Holy Spirit', i.e., confirmed them. In the same way, after you have been carefully instructed and prepared, the Bishop comes and 'lays his hands' upon you, and *you receive the Holy Spirit*. The word 'confirmation', a convenient name for this, came later. The word means 'strengthening'.

Confirmation: The Promises

At your Baptism (if in infancy) godparents made promises on your behalf. At Confirmation you make these promises yourself. You shoulder the responsibility because you are now a responsible person. But it is one thing to make a promise—it is quite another to keep that promise. You need special help, God's help. The Church calls it 'grace', strength greater than your own, power from the Holy Spirit. That power is given you at Confirmation, the laying on of hands being the outward visible sign. But it is neither automatic nor magic. You must call on that power and use it. It's rather like a cheque—little good to you till you cash it. Just having it in your pocket won't keep you from hunger.

When you are conFIRMed you make firm those promises, and are made firm to keep them by the grace and strength given you.

Confirmation: Strength for Living

Think of Confirmation as your special ordination or equipping with strength by God for your life's work. As the Sovereign when anointed at coronation is given grace to rule, or a bishop at his consecration is given grace for his high office, so you at Confirmation are given grace for your life's work, which is to fight under Christ's banner against sin, the world and the Devil and to continue Christ's faithful soldier and servant unto your life's end.

Confirmation: A Beginning

In this way Confirmation continues the process begun at Baptism. But it must not end it. That strength of the Holy Spirit given at Confirmation must be fed regularly all through your life by the Holy Communion.

THE DUTIES OF A
CHURCHMAN

A Christian must live a life of discipline. Certain things are *duties*—a word not liked nowadays. They must be done always—whether we feel in the mood or not. It is by drilling ourselves to do these things that the strength of character necessary for resisting temptation is won. But we cannot do this alone in our own strength. We can do it only with God's help. The secret is to remember our Lord's presence, the power of his Holy Spirit, 'the One who stands by to help'. This power has been given to us and we must learn to call on and trust him whose strength is sufficient for us. Because a Christian knows he is never alone and practises the presence of Christ, he will be a happy, cheerful person, never downcast for long. He will be kind in his remarks and judgments about other people, always looking for the best in others. In Jesus' company (and we are in his company) we should be ashamed to say or think a mean thing, nor should we grumble or be gloomy.

So the duties of a Churchman, which help us to know Christ's presence, lead us to inward peace, quietness, and joy. We shall have the royalty of inward happiness.

These are the duties of a Churchman:

DUTY TO GOD

Worship

This is the foundation on which all else is built. By Jesus' own example in attending his place of worship, the synagogue, week by week, and also because we are told plainly in the Bible, we know that worship is the first duty of a Christian.

'Worship' means 'making God of most worth'.

The Holy Communion is the most important act of the Church's worship. Every Churchman should put it first in obedience to our Lord's command, 'DO THIS in remembrance of me'.

Prayer

Our Lord often rose a great while before the day to have enough time in his busy life for prayer. A Christian should always begin the day with prayer, and be in touch with his Heavenly Father again before he goes to bed at night. He will practise the presence of Christ, that is, remember that our Lord is with him all the time; and he will often send little 'arrow prayers'—messages of thanks, or love, or calls for help—winging their way to him.

Bible Reading

Daily reading of the Bible is far more important to a Christian than reading the daily papers. The Bible is the Christian's daily *good* news. It is one of the vital links between God and man. Read carefully about this on page 37.

Self-discipline

'The good which I want to do, I fail to do; but what I do is the wrong which is against my will,' said St Paul. Even he had a fight to rule himself. 'Every athlete goes into strict training. They do it to win a fading wreath; we, a wreath that never fades. For my part, I run with a clear goal before me; I am like a boxer who does not beat the air; I bruise my own body and make it know its master.'

Mastery over self is won only by constant self-discipline, and the greatest help to this is the keeping of our rule of life; that is, the rules we make for ourselves about our prayers, worship, Communion, reading of the Bible, etc.

'Fasting' is a useful aid towards this self-discipline. It means self-control in our eating, learning to deny ourselves certain foods. For example, it has for long been a custom of the Church to abstain from eating meat on Friday, the day of our Lord's Crucifixion, and on the main fast days of the Christian Year, that we may be reminded of his sacrifice for us. He did so much for us. We can surely do a little thing like that in acknowledgement.

Almsgiving

None of our possessions are *really* ours. God allows us the use of them. We are only stewards. This is particularly true of our money. We must put it to the best and most unselfish use.

(a) We must decide how much we ought to give to the upkeep of our Church. A regular payment system like the stewardship envelope is much better than the haphazard coin in the plate. But supporting our Church is not *giving*. It is only *paying* for what we need, just as we pay for food or clothing. It is a debt of honour, because no bill is sent.

(b) Mission is a direct command of Jesus: 'Go ye, teach all nations and baptize them'. Many can obey only by giving and by prayer.

(c) Good causes make a claim on Christian generosity. Fighting hunger and disease in many lands; care of the aged, sick or homeless; helping young and old through clubs, etc.; etc.

DUTY TO OUR NEIGHBOUR

Service

We are stewards not only of our money but also of our abilities and of our time. These must be used, not only for our own enjoyment, but for the good of others. So a Christian seeks ways in which to serve. The method matters little so long as we are giving of ourselves for the benefit of others. One may teach in a Sunday school, another may run a Guide company, a third may sit at home to release a parent to get out for a little relaxation. We give invaluable service by being dependable and regular in any organization to which we belong. There are also civic and social duties, vital fields of service, neglect of which has weakened the Church.

These duties are summed up in this

Short Guide to the
Duties of Church Membership

*Authorized by the
Archbishops of Canterbury and York*

All baptized and confirmed members of the Church must play their full part in its life and witness. That you may fulfil this duty we call upon you:

To follow the example of Christ in home and daily life, and to bear personal witness to him.

To be regular in private prayer day by day.

To read the Bible carefully.

To come to church every Sunday.

To receive the Holy Communion faithfully and regularly.

To give personal service to Church, neighbours and community.

To give money for the work of the parish and diocese and for the work of the Church at home and overseas.

To uphold the standard of marriage entrusted by Christ to his Church.

To care that children are brought up to love and serve the Lord.

THE CHURCH'S BOOKS

I. THE BIBLE

'The most valuable thing this world affords' is how the Archbishop of Canterbury describes the Bible when, at the coronation of our Sovereigns in Westminster Abbey, he hands the Holy Scriptures to the Monarch. Yet an American journalist could give the title *The Book Nobody Knows* to a book he wrote about the Bible. The most valuable thing this world affords—the book nobody knows. Can this be so? Certainly few today know it as well as earlier generations and the whole nation is thereby poorer.

Why Is the Bible so Valuable?

(1) Because it is the record, divinely inspired, of God's dealings with mankind. The Old Testament traces the ways in which God revealed his nature to men and women, and tried to make them understand his laws, what he required from them, and his love for rich and poor alike.

The Old Testament shows how the way was prepared over the centuries for the coming into the world of Jesus Christ.

The New Testament contains four lives of Jesus (the Gospels), or more correctly, accounts of his ministry; a history of the earliest days of the Church (the Acts of the Apostles); and letters from the Apostles to congregations they had established, or to men and women who had been their friends in this work (the Epistles).

(2) Because the study of the Bible—the reading of a passage, imagining it all, and then thinking over

37

carefully what it means for us today—is one of God's appointed ways of speaking in our hearts, and making his will known.

Why 'The Book Nobody Knows'?

The Bible is not simply a book, but rather a library, for there are sixty-six books (not counting the section called the Apocrypha). The oldest books in the Old Testament were written seven or eight hundred years B.C. (before the birth of Christ); the New Testament all in the first century A.D. (Anno Domini, in the year of our Lord, i.e., since the Birth of Christ). People so long ago had different ways of thought and fashions of speech. They would have been as puzzled by our ways as we today find theirs difficult and misleading.

Then, too, the books of the Bible have been translated out of their original Hebrew or other ancient tongues.

The translation once used in all churches, the 'Authorized Version', was made over 300 years ago at the command of James I. But words develop rather different meanings over such a long period. Clearly we need all the help we can get if we are to have the greatest benefit from this 'most valuable thing the world affords'.

Nowadays most churches use new translations in up-to-date English, such as the New English Bible, the Jerusalem Bible, the Revised Standard Version, the Good News Bible or the New International Version. You should have one of these for your own use too; they are available in a wide variety of editions ranging from the very expensive to the cheap paperback.

How to Read the Bible

How much of the Bible you read is not nearly so important as *how you read it*. Offer a prayer first that God may speak to you through the passage chosen. Then read very slowly, making a great effort of imagination. Picture the scene, 'get inside' what you are reading, feel yourself there and taking part. Try to apply it to yourself. What is the message for you? Probably you will want to say a prayer about it.

All this is an art—it needs practice. Don't be disappointed if you do not get on too well at first. Persevere.

Join the Bible Reading Fellowship

To help you read your Bible regularly, the Bible Reading Fellowship publish a number of quarterly booklets. 'Awake to the Word' and 'Brief Notes' give a short explanation of the passage set and a suggestion of how it applies to your own life. 'Compass' and 'Discovery', for children and young people, each week give stories and ideas of things to do to help your Bible reading come to life. Ask your priest about it. He will strongly approve. The address of the B.R.F. is St Michael's House, 2 Elizabeth Street, London SW1W 9RQ.

II. THE PRAYER BOOK AND THE ALTERNATIVE SERVICE BOOK 1980

Before the Reformation, all church services were in Latin and contained in a number of different books. So, after the break with Rome, Archbishop Cranmer decided that all churches throughout the land should follow the same service and use just one book. He rewrote the old services in the common language so that more people could understand them, and altered them so that they were closer to what he believed the worship of the early Church had been.

Cranmer's book, the Book of Common Prayer, was taken by English people throughout the world and forms the basis for all the different prayer books used by the Churches of the worldwide Anglican Communion.

In England, however, the Prayer Book was last revised as long ago as 1662, and has never been replaced; but in 1980 a new book called The Alternative Service Book 1980 was published. This contains most of the services to be found in the Prayer Book but rewritten—just as Cranmer did in the sixteenth century—in modern English and in the light of our further knowledge about the services of the early Church. The balance between the old and the new, which the Church of England has traditionally sought to maintain, is now expressed by the use of two alternative books—the Prayer Book and the ASB.

The monks had seven 'Hours' of prayer—services or 'offices' said or sung every day. Out of these Cranmer constructed Mattins and Evensong, two services of psalms, readings and prayers, to be the daily prayer of the Church. The ASB contains shorter forms of both

Morning and Evening Prayer, which are ideal for use at home, as well as longer versions in modern English for use in church.

The Holy Communion (or the Eucharist) is everywhere the heart of the Church's worship, and probably the service you know best. In the ASB there are two versions, one in modern English (Rite A) and one in more traditional language (Rite B).

You will also find there the special prayers, 'collects', and readings from the Old and New Testaments and the Gospels for every Sunday and Holy Day of the Christian Year. When you cannot be at church on a Holy Day make a practice of reading at home the collect and readings appointed.

Both the Prayer Book and the ASB contain other great offices: Baptism, when we enter the Church, and Confirmation, when we are strengthened for our life's work; the Marriage service, when God gives men and women grace to live in a special union which should be holy; the Funeral service, when the Church lays to rest the bodies of those who have died.

The Ordinal contains the forms of service when men are ordained for the Ministry, as deacons, priests or bishops.

The Prayer Book and many editions of the ASB also contain the Psalms, the hymn-book of the Jews, which Jesus often quoted and must have known by heart.

THE CHURCH'S YEAR

The Church Calendar begins with five 'Sundays before Christmas' leading up to

ADVENT SUNDAY

(either the last Sunday in November or the first in December).

There are four Sundays in Advent and during this period the Church prepares for

CHRISTMAS

the celebration of the Birthday or First Coming of Jesus when he was born at Bethlehem, and the Son of God became man.

EPIPHANY

commemorates the revealing ('showing forth' is the exact meaning of the word) of the Divine Nature, first to the Wise Men from the East. It is observed on 6 January. There are one to six Sundays after Epiphany. Then three 'Sundays before Easter' give warning of

ASH WEDNESDAY

(preceded by Shrove Tuesday, when people confessed their sins), which is the first day of

LENT

This solemn period of discipline, repentance and growth lasts roughly forty days, the period of our Lord's special preparation in the wilderness for the opening of his Ministry. The fourth Sunday in Lent is often kept as Mothering Sunday. The fifth Sunday in Lent is called Passion Sunday. Next comes Palm Sunday, when Jesus entered into Jerusalem for the final week of teaching in the Temple, known as

HOLY WEEK

which led up to the Last Supper, on Maundy Thursday evening, immediately before he went to the Garden of Gethsemane. There he was betrayed, and taken away for trial before the High Priest in the early morning and afterwards condemned by Pontius Pilate, the Roman Governor. He was crucified later that day, called

GOOD FRIDAY

He rose from the grave on the first day of the week,

EASTER DAY

and of this event every Sunday is the commemoration week by week.

There follow the great Forty Days, when Christ appeared frequently to the disciples and others, teaching and preparing them. He withdrew his bodily presence on

ASCENSION DAY

which, being the fortieth day after Easter, always falls on a Thursday. As Christ had promised, after ten days of waiting and prayer in the Upper Room in Jerusalem, the disciples received the Holy Spirit on

WHITSUNDAY OR PENTECOST

The Holy Spirit was to lead them into all truth and strengthen them for the colossal task of making Christ known to the uttermost parts of the earth, to all men, everywhere, in all ages. Whitsunday is often known as the Birthday of the Church. As the day of the original bestowing of the Holy Spirit, it was a favourite day for Baptism. A week later, on

TRINITY SUNDAY

the Church acknowledges the glory of the Eternal Trinity, Father, Son and Holy Spirit; and for the remaining twenty or so Sundays of the year, considers the great teachings and lessons of the faith once delivered. In these the Holy Spirit is ever leading us to perceive new depths of meaning, new relevancy for the changes and chances of the passing years and the developing social scene.

At the beginning of the Prayer Book is a Calendar showing the dates when the Church honours her heroes. The Apostles are each commemorated and also some of the greatest of the Saints, and all are remembered together on All Saints' Day. The Blessed Virgin Mary is honoured on several days, especially on 8 September, and with her Son at Candlemas (2 February) and the Annunciation or Lady Day (25 March).

On Michaelmas Day the Church reverences those higher ranks of God's creation, the Holy Angels.

THE CHURCH'S COLOURS

Each type of Festival and Fast has its distinctive colour—shown in the altar frontal, vestments, stole, pulpit fall and book markers. The colours thus announce the Church's Year.

These are the main colours and their meaning:

WHITE (or cream or gold): The joyful Festivals, especially Christmas, Easter and Ascension. Also for saints other than martyrs.

RED is the colour of fire and blood, so is used for Whitsunday and for martyrs.

VIOLET (or purple) speaks of penitence and preparation—so is used in Lent and Advent.

GREEN, the ordinary colour of nature, suggests God's provision for our needs—so green is for ordinary, non-festival Sundays.

THE CHURCH'S CLOTHES:
THE VESTMENTS

Distinctive dress for various functions is worn in many callings. Not many have as long a history as church vestments, which are adaptations of the classical costumes of the Roman Empire. As styles went out of fashion for everyday wear they were retained in church use, and with modification have come down to us today. In the illustrations you will see the main vestments, and below is a list of their names and uses.

ALB—long white linen garment reaching to the ankles, derived from ancient tunic.

AMICE—once a neckcloth, has now become a linen square worn round the neck to protect the other vestments. Often decorated with an apparel.

APPARELS—ornamental panels at the foot of the alb, front and back, and on amice.

CASSOCK—the long black gown worn under other vestments. It used to be the day-to-day working costume of the clergy, not merely used in church. Some are again wearing it for day-to-day use. A bishop's cassock is purple, symbolic of rank.

CHASUBLE—worn by priest or bishop when celebrating the Holy Communion. It is descended from the commonest outdoor garment of classical times.

CHIMERE—of black or scarlet, open in front, worn by bishops over the rochet.

COPE—in the pre-Christian era it was a long cloak. It has become a costly embroidered vestment worn by bishops on occasions such as Confirmations or Ordinations, and by priests in Processions on Festivals, etc.

A Surplice
B Scarf
C Cassock
D Hood

Priest in choir dress

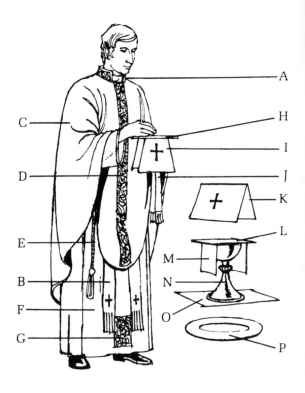

A Amice	E Girdle	I Veil	M Purificator
B Stole	F Alb	J Maniple	N Chalice
C Chasuble	G Apparel	K Burse	O Corporal
D Orphrey	H Burse	L Pall	P Paten

Priest in Eucharistic vestments

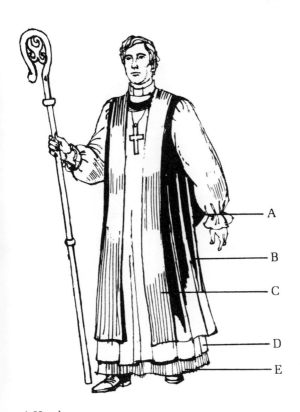

A Hood

B Chimere

C Scarf   D Rochet   E Cassock

Bishop in rochet and chimere

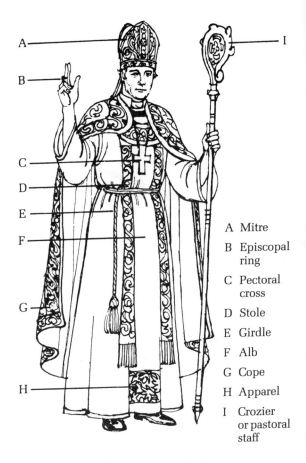

A Mitre

B Episcopal ring

C Pectoral cross

D Stole

E Girdle

F Alb

G Cope

H Apparel

I Crozier or pastoral staff

Bishop in cope and mitre

COTTA—similar to surplice, but shorter, especially in the sleeves. Sometimes used by clergy and servers in place of surplice.

GIRDLE—a cord used to secure the alb or cassock round the waist.

HOOD—worn by clergy at choir offices (Mattins and Evensong, etc.). Was a medieval head-dress, as name implies, but now worn hanging down the back. It denotes a university degree. Each has its distinctive colour.

MANIPLE—originally a napkin. It is worn over the left arm by bishops, priests and deacons at the Eucharist. It probably came into church use to cleanse the vessels after the stole had developed as described below.

MITRE—the head-dress of a bishop. Mitres are tongue-shaped and remind us of the tongues of fire which lighted on the Apostles at Pentecost.

ORPHREYS—the embroidered strips, usually cross-shaped, on a chasuble.

ROCHET—worn by bishops. It is like an alb, but is used without girdle or apparels.

STOLE—was once a napkin or towel carried by servants on the left shoulder. It became folded and narrow. As the deacons' duty was to cleanse the sacred vessels they wear it over the left shoulder. Priests wear the stole over both shoulders. The stole is worn at all the Sacraments.

SURPLICE—of white linen, reaching to the knees. Is worn by choir and servers as well as clergy.

TIPPET—the black scarf worn with the hood at the choir offices, etc.

PART III:
THE HOLY COMMUNION

WHAT IS
THE HOLY COMMUNION?

On the night Jesus was betrayed to his enemies and taken to be crucified, at the last supper with his friends in that upper room in Jerusalem, he gave thanks and broke bread which he blessed and they all shared, and he said: 'This is my body which is given for you. Do this in remembrance of me.' And he blessed wine and said: 'Drink this, all of you; this is my blood of the new covenant, which is shed for you and for many for the forgiveness of sins. Do this, as often as you shall drink it, in remembrance of me.'

The Jews were used to a ceremonial meal as part of their worship of God, and Jesus at the Last Supper gave his friends a direct command which they could appreciate and obey. From that day to this the Sacrament of the Lord's Supper has been the central act of worship of the Church. It is known by at least six names: The Lord's Supper, The Holy Communion, The Holy Eucharist, The Blessed Sacrament (of the Body and Blood of Christ), The Mass, The Liturgy.

The Holy Communion is a Sacrament, the 'outward and visible sign of an inward and spiritual grace given unto us', in this way. The outward and visible sign is the Bread and Wine, blessed with the very words Jesus himself spoke in the upper room. The inward and spiritual grace given us is the divine life of Christ himself, grace, a share in the very nature of God. We are united with Christ, and his Spirit and Nature flow into us.

There are two parts of the Holy Communion: what man does; what God does.

What Man Does

The Holy Communion is a sacrifice, that is, a gift which people offer to God through their appointed priest, as a sign of their dependence on God, and in acknowledgement of God's absolute power and authority over them. 'We offer you our souls and bodies to be a living sacrifice through Jesus Christ our Lord.'

But we dare not offer anything so marred and sinful as we are except through Jesus Christ; that is, by joining our unworthy offering to his perfect offering of himself, spotless and sinless.

What God Does

God accepts the offering of our sinful and unworthy selves because we unite our self-offering with the perfect offering of Jesus on Calvary. He gives to us through the Bread and Wine the divine life of Jesus, his 'grace and heavenly blessing'. He assures us of our membership with all the rest of the Church, both that part of it kneeling with us at those altar rails and other parts everywhere throughout the earth, as well as those departed from this world and now in the life beyond.

In the Holy Communion, everything in human life—our work, our homes, our love, our pleasure, leisure, hopes, fears, griefs, joys, our studies, ideas, successes, our sacrifices—all can be offered to God through Christ. All are represented in the Bread and Wine. God takes them up and consecrates them and gives them back together with the gift of divine life, so that in these things of daily life we can glorify and serve him.

Here is how a modern Prayer Book Catechism (the Canadian) puts it:

Question Why was the Sacrament of the Lord's Supper ordained?

Answer For the continual remembrance of the sacrifice of the death of Christ, and of the benefits which we receive thereby.

Question What is the outward part or sign of the Lord's Supper?

Answer Bread and Wine, which the Lord hath commanded to be received.

Question What is the inward part, or thing signified?

Answer The Body and Blood of Christ, which are verily and indeed taken and received by the faithful in the Lord's Supper.

Question What benefits do we receive thereby?

Answer The strengthening and refreshing of our souls and bodies unto eternal life by the Body and Blood of Christ.

All this is a mystery none can fully understand. It is enough that Jesus commanded us, 'Do this in remembrance of me.' To that command Christ's followers will always be faithful. If we come to Communion carefully prepared, although we shall not at first perceive all that is contained in that wonderful Sacrament—no one does—we shall find it a great source of strength, comfort and happiness.

We shall come at first because we know it is our duty and we rejoice to obey. It will not be very long before we come because we have learnt to find Jesus there, nearer than at any other time, and nothing will then keep us away from being in his Presence.

HOW OFTEN SHALL I MAKE
MY COMMUNION?

You must decide this for yourself. Be sure of two points:

(1) **Have a rule** about how often you go, and keep it.

(2) **Always prepare** thoroughly before making your Communion.

Whether you decide that it shall be every Sunday (which should be your ultimate aim), or whether you decide at first to receive the Blessed Sacrament fortnightly or monthly, is a matter you should discuss with your priest.

There are in addition 'Days of Obligation' when every communicant should be present:

Easter Day; Christmas Day; Whitsunday; Ascension Day.

Make a special point of attending on Ash Wednesday, the first day of Lent; and Maundy Thursday, the day of the Last Supper and therefore the anniversary of the institution of Holy Communion.

Come on special weekdays, too, if you can, such as Feasts of the Apostles, Lady Day, Michaelmas Day, All Saints' Day, your own birthday or other special anniversary, e.g., the anniversary of your wedding, Confirmation, or the birthday or day of the death of ones whom you love.

Would a regular weekday morning before going to work be possible? Bring to our Lord your cares and worries and also your thanksgivings and praise.

Remember: you do not need to receive Holy Communion every time you come.

OUR PREPARATION FOR HOLY COMMUNION

The essential things are

TO KNOW PRECISELY

what you are going to

GIVE THANKS FOR

CONFESS

PRAY FOR

Vagueness is the curse of religion. The road to hell is paved with good intentions, the things we vaguely meant to do—but of course didn't. So be very definite and clear-cut.

Think out the night before your Communion, or earlier, just exactly what you will thank God for, what you must confess, the subject for which chiefly you will pray, pleading with God for this special and particular thing, or person, the sacrifice of Jesus on the Cross. This chief subject of our praying is known as our SPECIAL INTENTION.

Go to Holy Communion so prepared that, were anyone suddenly to ask you as you entered the doors of the church, 'What are you going to THANK God for this morning?' without a moment's hesitation you could answer. In the same way, supposing you were suddenly asked 'What are you going to CONFESS to God this morning?' you could reply instantly. Or, again, if you were asked 'What is your INTENTION this morning?—that is to say, 'For what, or for whom, are you going to PRAY chiefly?'—at once you could give a definite answer.

That is the essence of a good preparation.

St Paul said:

'Anyone who eats the bread or drinks the cup of the Lord unworthily will be guilty of desecrating the body and blood of the Lord. A man must test himself before eating his share of the bread and drinking from the cup.'

DURING THE EUCHARIST

Because the Eucharist is not something done by the priest alone for the congregation but offered in Christ's name by all the people, it is important for each person to join fully in the celebration. Do this by following the service attentively, joining in the prayers said by all and saying 'Amen' or the appropriate response to the prayers led by the priest or one of the congregation. In this way you can make all the prayers your own.

Before the Service Begins

People usually kneel to pray before the Holy Communion service starts. Go over in your mind your preparation. Lay out ready, as it were, those things you decided to thank God for, to confess, and to pray for. Consider each carefully. Offer each to our Lord. Pray about them. Pray for the priest and all your fellow communicants in the church.

The Preparation and the Ministry of the Word

The Prayers of Penitence may be said towards the beginning of the service or after the Intercession.

Before saying the Confession and receiving God's forgiveness, briefly call to mind your sins and your desire to do better, 'to keep God's commandments and to live in love and peace with all men'.

Listen carefully to the Readings and reflect on them; some churches observe a helpful silence after each reading. Every Sunday there should be a sermon; this will help us understand the Readings more fully and enable us to proclaim the Gospel with more confidence in our daily lives.

The Ministry of the Sacrament

After we have shown our fellowship with one another at the Peace, the Bread and Wine are placed on the altar, and the priest may praise God for his gifts, saying:

> Blessed are you, Lord, God of all creation.
> Through your goodness we have this bread to offer, which earth has given and human hands have made.
> It will become for us the bread of life.

All   **Blessed be God for ever.**

Priest   Blessed are you, Lord, God of all creation.
> Through your goodness we have this wine to offer, fruit of the vine and work of human hands.
> It will become our spiritual drink.

All   **Blessed be God for ever.**

The Bread and Wine are things people have made. They represent our work, our whole life, and they are offered to God. At this point offer your whole work, all you do all day long, to God. Then thank him. The money you put in the plate is your acknowledgement that all you have depends on him. He can let you have it, or take it away. Offer him your thanksgivings for all you have and are.

After the Eucharistic Prayer, Christ is present, in the consecrated Bread and Wine. Before you receive Communion, *adore* him. Try to realize that he is there with you in the church, his house. Though unseen and invisible he is just as truly present. You cannot see the air, but you breathe it. This Communion is a meeting-place with your Lord.

Thee we adore, O hidden Saviour, thee,
Who in thy Sacrament dost deign to be;
Both Flesh and Spirit at thy Presence fail,
Yet here thy Presence we devoutly hail.

Pour out your love, your worship. Now is the time to pray about your special intention, the people or

matters you made ready at your preparation for this moment.

You go and kneel at the altar rails. Worship and adore your Saviour. Bring him again all that you decided in your preparation—your thanksgivings, confession, and special intercessions.

After the Communion

After you have received Communion, give thanks for the wonderful thing that has happened to you, for the precious gift of grace you have been given—that you have been with our Lord. From your confession there will likely arise a good resolution, e.g. if you have neglected your prayers, you must resolve most firmly to overcome this sin, and become faithful and regular in your praying. Make your resolution quite definite. It is the best possible way to thank our Lord.

Here is a summary:

Before the service begins: Go over your preparation. Lay out ready what you will thank God for, confess, pray for. Pray for the priest and the congregation.

At the Prayers of Penitence: Recall your sins and your sorrow for them.

At the Preparation of the Gifts: Give thanks and offer your daily life and work.

At the Communion: Worship Christ present in the Sacrament. Pray for your special intention.

After Communion: Give thanks for your Communion and make a good resolution.

Use this method Sunday by Sunday until it is your habit. It will help greatly.

PART IV:
THE FORGIVENESS OF SINS

HOW WE ARE FORGIVEN

Can you remember as a child getting into some scrape, and before you were forgiven having to go and tell your father you were sorry? It is the same in our religion. Before God forgives us our sins we must tell him we are sorry—we have to confess our sins. There are several things involved in this. First we must be truly sorry about our sins (and remember, the good we have failed to do, the prayers we have failed to offer, rank as sin just as much as the wrong or evil we have said or thought or done). It is more a matter of the *will* than of feelings, purposing with all the strength of character that we have to improve—to do the good we have previously failed to do, to avoid the evil. But we must ask and use God's help, because we cannot do it in your own strength. Having that intention we tell God how we have failed. He knows already, of course, but like every father he wants us to own up, and *face* up. Jesus taught us that then, when we have done this, God removes the guilt. We are forgiven.

There are two ways of confessing our sins. Both bring forgiveness when we really repent, really intend to do better.

The first way is privately—it may be either kneeling by our own bedside or it may be in church—telling God in our own words in secret what our sins have been, how firmly we mean to do better, and begging for forgiveness. When that is sincere God forgives. There is no doubt of that. We have Jesus' promise.

There are words to help in this in Evening Prayers on page 12.

The second way to confess our sins to God is in the presence of some 'discreet and learned minister of God's Word', who will give us advice and help 'to the quietening of our conscience and the avoidance of all scruple and doubtfulness', and then, acting as God's spokesman, assure us of God's forgiveness.

For more about this second way, see page 68.

Before using either we need to try to see ourselves as we must appear in God's sight. We take a rosy view of ourselves, and excuse ourselves too easily. We should, therefore, in self-examination, prod memory and conscience by questions designed to let us see ourselves more as God sees us and as we really are.

See below: Overhauling Ourselves; and page 64, Questions for Self-examination.

OVERHAULING OURSELVES

Each evening in our prayers we review what we have done or left undone in the day now past, and ask forgiveness for the sins revealed.

Before each Communion (be it weekly, fortnightly, or monthly, or on special Holy Days of the Church, or on our birthday), we require to examine ourselves more strictly—else we shall not know precisely what we must confess. And unless we know what we are asking forgiveness for, how can we expect God to forgive us? For we must come cleansed and forgiven to our Communion. This forgiveness is the 'wedding garment' Christ told us we must wear at the King's banquet. So questions for self-examination are provided on pages 65 to 67, and the instruction on Forgiveness, page 62.

Just as houses require spring-cleaning, so we need 'spring-cleaning', at least once a year, or probably more often. Before our Communion at the great Festivals, especially Easter and Christmas, is the best time for an extra special overhaul, to see whether we are advancing or falling back in our fight to become people on whom Christ can rely.

For this, use with care the questions which follow, especially if you have decided to seek 'comfort and counsel' from some 'discreet and learned minister of God's Word', as the Prayer Book puts it, in order to receive the 'benefit of absolution'.

Many who are trying hard to advance in service of our Lord and his Church have decided to do this if only for the spiritual counsel and advice received.

QUESTIONS FOR SELF-EXAMINATION

A good plan is to have paper and pencil and jot down the things we must confess. Just write single words, e.g. 'lying', jealousy', 'prayers missed'. You can put this paper in your prayer book and use it after you arrive in church in the minutes before the service begins, praying about these sins and asking for strength to overcome them. Having a paper ensures that you remember everything.

Kneel down. Think of our Lord on the Cross. Remember it was the wickedness and unlovingness of ordinary people like us which caused his death. Say a prayer such as this:

Holy Spirit, help me now to know the truth about myself. Stir up my conscience and memory that I may perceive how I have failed. Show me my sins against God and my sins against my fellows, the evil I have done and the good I have not done, so that I may truly repent and determine to do better and overcome my faults, with your help; for Jesus' sake.

The Things Left Undone

(Sins of Omission)

Have I omitted my morning prayers?—my evening prayers?—been careless in them?

Have I kept Sunday holy?

Have I stayed away from the Holy Communion on Sunday when I could have been there?

Have I prepared carefully before receiving Holy Communion?

Have I kept my rule about Bible reading?

Have I done what I ought and could—for the Church?—in my home?—for others?

Have I let slide a chance to do a kind act?—or say a kind word?—or stand up for my Faith?

Have I given as much money as I could afford for the work of the Church at home and overseas?

Have I really tried constantly to make God of most worth in my life?—or let dancing, the cinema, television, or lying in bed interfere with my duty to him?

The Things We Ought Not to Have Done

(Sins of Commission)

In Thought

Have I thought uncharitably about others?—been jealous?

Have I been conceited?—vain?—cocksure?—contemptuous?

Have I harboured malice or hatred in my heart?

Have I been spiteful?—unforgiving?

Have I let linger in my mind impure thoughts or imaginings, or desires?

In Word

Have I made fun of holy things?—spoken irreverently?—used God's name lightly?

Have I used bad language?—told dirty jokes?

Have I been strictly truthful?

Have I gossiped?—slandered others?—spoken unkindly about others?—boasted?

In Deed

Have I done my best at my work?

Have I stolen?—cheated?—delayed to pay my debts?—broken my word?

Have I been bad-tempered?—grumbled?—quarrelled?

Have I been greedy?—eaten or drunk more than my share or more than I needed?

Have I treated women and girls honourably, chivalrously and politely?—or tried to be smart?—to show off?

Have I made boys respect me?—or have I lowered the dignity of womanhood?

Have I been pure and clean and healthy in all that I do alone?—with others?

Have I taught evil to another?—set a bad example?—at home?—at work?—with my friends?

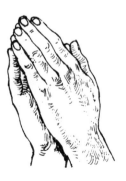

CONFESSION

To reach even a low standard of Christian living means a hard struggle. We are conscious of besetting sins which get the better of us constantly. We long for help in overcoming them. We know that our Lord is calling us not to a minimum standard but to holiness. How are we to attain it? Sometimes, too, old sins worry us. We do not feel 'right' with God.

The Prayer Book puts it this way: 'If there be any of you who by this means (i.e., private confession) cannot quiet his own conscience herein, but requireth further comfort or counsel, let him come to me or to some other discreet and learned minister of God's Word, and open his grief; that by the ministry of God's Holy Word he may receive the benefit of absolution, together with spiritual counsel and advice ...'

The Church makes available to us skilled advice to help us in life's battle. Just as ailments of the body show symptoms which a doctor is trained to recognize and treat, so a priest who is a good director is trained to recognize the ailments of the soul and treat them through the 'spiritual counsel and advice' he gives.

Two good reasons, therefore, given us in the Prayer Book for seeking this help are:

(1) The counsel and advice a wise priest can give which can help so greatly.

(2) The certainty of forgiveness and the joy this brings.

Should you decide to ask your priest to advise you in this way the times when he is available are sometimes made known in church or on the notice-board, or you may prefer to seek him in his own house. He will be very happy to help you. Or, if you prefer, you may go to a priest who is a stranger—'Come to me or to some other discreet and learned minister,' the Prayer Book says.

When you have talked to the priest he may ask you to kneel and use this form of words:

Priest   The Lord be in thy heart and on thy lips that thou mayest faithfully and truly confess thy sins unto him, to the honour and glory of his holy Name.

You now say:

I confess to God Almighty, the Father, the Son and the Holy Ghost and before the whole company of heaven, and to you, my father, that I have sinned exceedingly in thought, word, and deed, through my own grievous fault.

Especially I have sinned in these ways ....

(Here name all the sins you can remember. Refer to the list you made at your self-examination.)

For these and all my other sins which I cannot now remember, I am very sorry. I intend to lead a new life. I humbly ask pardon of God, and of you, my father, counsel and absolution.

The priest will give you advice. Then he will pronounce God's forgiveness in the Prayer Book words:

Our Lord Jesus Christ who hath left power to his Church to absolve all sinners who truly repent and believe in him, of his great mercy forgive thee thine offences; and by his authority committed unto me, I absolve thee from all thy sins, in the name of the Father, and of the Son, and of the Holy Ghost. *Amen.*

And he may add:

The Passion of our Lord Jesus Christ and his infinite merits be to thee for remission of sins, for growth in grace, and for the reward of everlasting life.

The Blessing of God Almighty, the Father, the Son, and the Holy Ghost, be with you now and evermore. *Amen.*

Go in peace. The Lord hath put away thy sins from thee.

Thank God with all your heart for his wonderful generosity and kindness in thus forgiving you.

THE
HOLY COMMUNION
according to

RITE A
The Alternative Service Book 1980

NOTES

Sections not preceded by the symbol ▶ may be omitted.

Texts in bold type are to be said or sung by the congregation.

The numbers [ASB/119], etc., indicate the corresponding page in The Alternative Service Book 1980.

THE PREPARATION

1.   At the entry of the ministers *AN APPROPRIATE*
    SENTENCE may be used; and A HYMN, A CANTICLE,
    or A PSALM may be sung.

2.   *The president welcomes the people using these or other*
    appropriate words.

             The Lord be with you *or* The Lord is here.

All   **and also with you.**   **His Spirit is with us.**

    or Easter Day to Pentecost

             Alleluia! Christ is risen.

All   **He is risen indeed. Alleluia!**

3.   *This prayer may be said.*

All   **Almighty God,**
             to whom all hearts are open,
             all desires known,
             and from whom no secrets are hidden:
             cleanse the thoughts of our hearts
             by the inspiration of your Holy Spirit,
             that we may perfectly love you,
             and worthily magnify your holy name;
             through Christ our Lord. Amen.

PRAYERS OF PENITENCE

4. *THE PRAYERS OF PENITENCE (sections 5-8) may be said here, or after section 23; if they are said here, sections 6-8 are always used. Alternative confessions may be used (see section 80).*

5. *THE COMMANDMENTS (section 78) or the following SUMMARY OF THE LAW may be said.*

Minister   Our Lord Jesus Christ said: The first commandment is this: 'Hear, O Israel, the Lord our God is the only Lord. You shall love the Lord your God with all your heart, with all your soul, with all your mind, and with all your strength.'
The second is this: 'Love your neighbour as yourself.' There is no other commandment greater than these.

All   **Amen. Lord, have mercy.**

▶6. *The minister invites the congregation to confess their sins in these or other suitable words (see section 25).*

God so loved the world that he gave his only Son Jesus Christ to save us from our sins, to be our advocate in heaven, and to bring us to eternal life.

Let us confess our sins, in penitence and faith, firmly resolved to keep God's commandments and to live in love and peace with all men.

▶7. **All**   **Almighty God, our heavenly Father,
we have sinned against you and against
    our fellow men,
in thought and word and deed,
through negligence, through weakness,
through our own deliberate fault.**

We are truly sorry
and repent of all our sins.

For the sake of your Son Jesus Christ, who
    died for us,
forgive us all that is past;
and grant that we may serve you in
    newness of life
to the glory of your name. Amen.

8. President   Almighty God,
who forgives all who truly repent,
have mercy upon you,
pardon and deliver you from all your sins,
confirm and strengthen you in all
    goodness,
and keep you in life eternal;
through Jesus Christ our Lord. **Amen.**

9. *KYRIE ELEISON may be said (see also section 79).*

Lord, have mercy.
Lord, have mercy.

Christ, have mercy.
Christ, have mercy.

Lord, have mercy.
Lord, have mercy.

10. *GLORIA IN EXCELSIS may be said.*

All   **Glory to God in the highest,
and peace to his people on earth.**

**Lord God, heavenly King,
almighty God and Father,
we worship you, we give you thanks,
we praise you for your glory.**

**Lord Jesus Christ, only Son of the Father,
Lord God, Lamb of God,
you take away the sin of the world:
have mercy on us;**

you are seated at the right hand of the
    Father:
receive our prayer.

For you alone are the Holy One,
you alone are the Lord,
you alone are the Most High,
Jesus Christ,
with the Holy Spirit,
in the glory of God the Father. Amen.

▶11.   *The president says THE COLLECT.*

THE MINISTRY OF THE WORD

▶12.   *Either two or three readings from scripture follow, the*
    last of which is always the Gospel.

13.   **Sit.** *OLD TESTAMENT READING.*
    At the end the reader may say

                This is the word of the Lord.
    All   **Thanks be to God.**

14.   *A PSALM may be used.*

15.   **Sit.** *NEW TESTAMENT READING (EPISTLE).*
    At the end the reader may say

                This is the word of the Lord.
    All   **Thanks be to God.**

16.   *A CANTICLE, A HYMN, or A PSALM may be used.*

▶ 17. **Stand.** *THE GOSPEL. When it is announced*

       All   **Glory to Christ our Saviour.**

At the end the reader says

              This is the Gospel of Christ.
       All   **Praise to Christ our Lord.**

▶ 18. **Sit.** *THE SERMON*

▶ 19. **Stand.** *THE NICENE CREED is said on Sundays and other Holy Days, and may be said on other days.*

       All   **We believe in one God,**
               the Father, the almighty,
               maker of heaven and earth,
               of all that is,
               seen and unseen.

               We believe in one Lord, Jesus Christ,
               the only Son of God,
               eternally begotten of the Father,
               God from God, Light from Light,
               true God from true God,
               begotten, not made,
               of one Being with the Father.
               Through him all things were made.
               For us men and for our salvation
               he came down from heaven;
               by the power of the Holy Spirit
               he became incarnate of the Virgin Mary,
                  and was made man.
               For our sake he was crucified under
                  Pontius Pilate;
               he suffered death and was buried.

               On the third day he rose again
               in accordance with the Scriptures;
               he ascended into heaven
               and is seated at the right hand of the
                  Father.

He will come again in glory
to judge the living and the dead,
and his kingdom will have no end.

We believe in the Holy Spirit,
the Lord, the giver of life,
who proceeds from the Father and the Son.
With the Father and the Son he is
     worshipped and glorified.
He has spoken through the Prophets.

We believe in one holy catholic
     and apostolic Church.
We acknowledge one baptism for the
     forgiveness of sins.
We look for the resurrection of the dead,
and the life of the world to come. Amen.

THE INTERCESSION

▶20.   *INTERCESSIONS AND THANKSGIVINGS are led by
        the president, or by others. The form below, or one of
        those in section 81, or other suitable words, may be
        used.*

21.   *This form may be used (a) with the insertion of specific
        subjects between the paragraphs; (b) as a continuous
        whole with or without brief biddings. Not all
        paragraphs need be used on every occasion. Individual
        names may be added at the places indicated. This
        response may be used before or after each paragraph.*

        Minister   Lord, in your mercy
        All   **hear our prayer.**

                   Let us pray for the Church and for the
                   world, and let us thank God for his
                   goodness.

Almighty God, our heavenly Father, you promised through your Son Jesus Christ to hear us when we pray in faith.

Strengthen N our bishop and all your Church in the service of Christ; that those who confess your name may be united in your truth, live together in your love, and reveal your glory in the world.

Bless and guide Elizabeth our Queen; give wisdom to all in authority; and direct this and every nation in the ways of justice and of peace; that men may honour one another, and seek the common good.

Give grace to us, our families and friends, and to all our neighbours; that we may serve Christ in one another, and love as he loves us.

Comfort and heal all those who suffer in body, mind, or spirit...; give them courage and hope in their troubles; and bring them the joy of your salvation.

Hear us as we remember those who have died in the faith of Christ...; according to your promises, grant us with them a share in your eternal kingdom.

Rejoicing in the fellowship of (N and of) all your saints, we commend ourselves and all Christian people to your unfailing love.

Merciful Father,

All   **accept these prayers**
for the sake of your Son,
our Saviour Jesus Christ. Amen.

▶ 22. *The Order following the pattern of the Book of Common Prayer continues at section 57.*

PRAYERS OF PENITENCE

23. *THE PRAYERS OF PENITENCE (sections 24-28) are said here, if they have not been said after section 4; if they are said here, sections 26-28 are always used. Alternative confessions may be used (see section 80).*

24. *THE COMMANDMENTS (section 78) or the following SUMMARY OF THE LAW may be said.*

Minister   Our Lord Jesus Christ said: The first commandment is this: 'Hear, O Israel, the Lord our God is the only Lord. You shall love the Lord your God with all your heart, with all your soul, with all your mind, and with all your strength.'
The second is this: 'Love your neighbour as yourself.' There is no other commandment greater than these.

All   **Amen. Lord, have mercy.**

25. *The minister may say*

God so loved the world that he gave his only Son Jesus Christ to save us from our sins, to be our advocate in heaven, and to bring us to eternal life.

or one or more of these SENTENCES.

Hear the words of comfort our Saviour Christ says to all who truly turn to him:
Come to me, all who labour and are heavy laden, and I will give you rest.
Matthew 11.28

God so loved the world that he gave his only Son, that whoever believes in him should not perish but have eternal life.
John 3.16

Hear what Saint Paul says: This saying is true and worthy of full acceptance, that Christ Jesus came into the world to save sinners. *1 Timothy 1.15*

Hear what Saint John says: If anyone sins, we have an advocate with the Father, Jesus Christ the righteous; and he is the propitiation for our sins. *1 John 2.1*

▶ 26. Minister   Let us confess our sins, in penitence and faith, firmly resolved to keep God's commandments and to live in love and peace with all men.

▶ 27. All

Almighty God, our heavenly Father,
we have sinned against you and against
   our fellow men,
in thought and word and deed,
through negligence, through weakness,
through our own deliberate fault.
We are truly sorry,
and repent of all our sins.
For the sake of your Son Jesus Christ, who
   died for us,
forgive us all that is past;
and grant that we may serve you in
   newness of life
to the glory of your name. Amen.

▶ 28. President

Almighty God,
who forgives all who truly repent,
have mercy upon you,
pardon and deliver you from all your sins,
confirm and strengthen you in all
   goodness,
and keep you in life eternal;
through Jesus Christ our Lord. **Amen.**

29. *All may say*

We do not presume
to come to this your table, merciful Lord,
trusting in our own righteousness,
but in your manifold and great mercies.
We are not worthy
so much as to gather up the crumbs under
    your table.
But you are the same Lord
whose nature is always to have mercy.
Grant us therefore, gracious Lord,
so to eat the flesh of your dear son
    Jesus Christ
and to drink his blood,
that we may evermore dwell in him
and he in us. Amen.

The alternative prayer at section 82 may be used.

THE MINISTRY OF THE SACRAMENT

THE PEACE

▶ 30. **Stand.** *The president says either of the following or other suitable words (see section 83).*

Christ is our peace.
He has reconciled us to God
    in one body by the cross.
We meet in his name and share his peace.

or   We are the Body of Christ.
In the one Spirit we were all baptized into
    one body.
Let us then pursue all that makes for peace
and builds up our common life.

He then says

>The peace of the Lord be always with you

All **and also with you.**

31. *The president may say*

>Let us offer one another a sign of peace.

and all may exchange a sign of peace.

THE PREPARATION OF THE GIFTS

▶32. *The bread and wine are placed on the holy table.*

33. *The president may praise God for his gifts in appropriate words to which all respond*

>**Blessed be God for ever.**

34. *The offerings of the people may be collected and presented. These words may be used.*

>**Yours, Lord, is the greatness, the power,**
>**the glory, the splendour, and the majesty;**
>**for everything in heaven and on earth is**
>** yours.**
>**All things come from you,**
>**and of your own do we give you.**

35. *At the preparation of the gifts A HYMN may be sung.*

THE EUCHARISTIC PRAYER

THE TAKING OF THE BREAD AND CUP AND
THE GIVING OF THANKS

▶36. *The president takes the bread and cup into his hands*
and replaces them on the holy table.

▶37. *The president uses one of the four EUCHARISTIC*
PRAYERS which follow.

▶38. *FIRST EUCHARISTIC PRAYER*

President The Lord be with you   or The Lord is here.
All   and also with you.   His Spirit is with us.

President Lift up your hearts.
All   We lift them to the Lord.

President Let us give thanks to the Lord our God.
All   It is right to give him thanks and praise.

President It is indeed right,
it is our duty and our joy,
at all times and in all places
to give you thanks and praise,
holy Father, heavenly King,
almighty and eternal God,
through Jesus Christ your only Son our
   Lord.

For he is your living Word;
through him you have created all things
   from the beginning,
and formed us in your own image.

Through him you have freed us from the
   slavery of sin,
giving him to be born as man and to die
   upon the cross;
you raised him from the dead
and exalted him to your right hand on high.

Through him you have sent upon us
your holy and life-giving Spirit,
and made us a people for your own
  possession.

PROPER PREFACE, when appropriate (section 76)

Therefore with angels and archangels,
and with all the company of heaven,
we proclaim your great and glorious name,
for ever praising you and saying:

All　　**Holy, holy, holy, Lord,**
God of power and might,
heaven and earth are full of your glory.
Hosanna in the highest.

This ANTHEM may also be used.

Blessed is he who comes in the name of
** the Lord.**
Hosanna in the highest.

President　Accept our praises, heavenly Father,
through your Son our Saviour Jesus Christ;
and as we follow his example and obey
  his command,
grant that by the power of your Holy Spirit
these gifts of bread and wine
may be to us his body and his blood;

Who in the same night that he was
  betrayed,
took bread and gave you thanks;
he broke it and gave it to his disciples,
  saying,
Take, eat; this is my body which is given
  for you;
do this in remembrance of me.
In the same way, after supper
he took the cup and gave you thanks;
he gave it to them, saying,

Drink this, all of you;
this is my blood of the new covenant,
which is shed for you and for many for the
forgiveness of sins.
Do this, as often as you drink it,
in remembrance of me.

All   **Christ has died:**
Christ is risen:
Christ will come again.

President   Therefore, heavenly Father,
we remember his offering of himself
made once for all upon the cross,
and proclaim his mighty resurrection and
glorious ascension.
As we look for his coming in glory,
we celebrate with this bread and this cup
his one perfect sacrifice.

Accept through him, our great high priest,
this our sacrifice of thanks and praise;
and as we eat and drink these holy gifts
in the presence of your divine majesty,
renew us by your Spirit,
inspire us with your love,
and unite us in the body of your Son,
Jesus Christ our Lord.

Through him, and with him, and in him,
by the power of the Holy Spirit,
with all who stand before you in earth
and heaven,
we worship you, Father almighty,
in songs of everlasting praise:

All   **Blessing and honour and glory and power**
be yours for ever and ever. Amen.

Silence may be kept.
The service continues with THE LORD'S PRAYER at
section 42 on page 96.

President   The Lord be with you   or   The Lord is here.
All   **and also with you.   His Spirit is with us.**

President   Lift up your hearts.
All   **We lift them to the Lord.**

President   Let us give thanks to the Lord our God.
All   **It is right to give him thanks and praise.**

President   It is indeed right,
        it is our duty and our joy,
        at all times and in all places
        to give you thanks and praise,
        holy Father, heavenly King,
        almighty and eternal God,
        through Jesus Christ your only Son our
          Lord.

*The following may be omitted if a Proper Preface is
used.*

        For he is your living Word;
        through him you have created all things
            from the beginning,
        and formed us in your own image.

        Through him you have freed us from the
            slavery of sin,
        giving him to be born as man and to die
            upon the cross;
        you raised him from the dead
        and exalted him to your right hand on high.

        Through him you have sent upon us
        your holy and life-giving Spirit,
        and made us a people for your own
            possession.

PROPER PREFACE, when appropriate (section 76)

Therefore with angels and archangels,
and with all the company of heaven,
we proclaim your great and glorious name,
for ever praising you and saying:

All   **Holy, holy, holy Lord,**
God of power and might,
heaven and earth are full of your glory.
Hosanna in the highest.

This ANTHEM may also be used.

Blessed is he who comes in the name of
    the Lord.
Hosanna in the highest.

President   Hear us, heavenly Father,
through Jesus Christ your Son our Lord,
through him accept our sacrifice of praise;
and grant that by the power of your
    Holy Spirit
these gifts of bread and wine
may be to us his body and his blood;

Who in the same night that he was
    betrayed,
took bread and gave you thanks;
he broke it and gave it to his disciples,
    saying,
Take, eat; this in my body which is given
    for you;
do this in remembrance of me.
In the same way, after supper
he took the cup and gave you thanks;
he gave it to them, saying,
Drink this, all of you;
this is my blood of the new covenant,
which is shed for you and for many for the
    forgiveness of sins.
Do this, as often as you drink it,
in remembrance of me.

                                          [ASB/134]

All	**Christ has died:** **Christ is risen:** **Christ will come again.**

President   Therefore, Lord and heavenly Father,
having in remembrance his death once for
    all upon the cross,
his resurrection from the dead,
and his ascension into heaven,
and looking for the coming of his kingdom,
we make with this bread and this cup
the memorial of Christ your Son our Lord.

Accept through him this offering of our
    duty and service;
and as we eat and drink these holy gifts
in the presence of your divine majesty,
fill us with your grace and heavenly
    blessing;
nourish us with the body and blood of your
    Son,
that we may grow into his likeness
and, made one by your Spirit,
become a living temple to your glory.

Through Jesus Christ our Lord,
by whom, and with whom, and in whom,
in the unity of the Holy Spirit,
all honour and glory be yours, almighty
    Father,
from all who stand before you in earth
    and heaven,
now and for ever. **Amen.**

Silence may be kept.

*The service continues with THE LORD'S PRAYER at
section 42 on page 96.*

THIRD EUCHARISTIC PRAYER

President	The Lord be with you *or* The Lord is here.
All	**and also with you.** **His Spirit is with us.**

President Lift up your hearts.
All   **We lift them to the Lord.**

President Let us give thanks to the Lord our God.
All   **It is right to give him thanks and praise.**

President Father, we give you thanks and praise
through your beloved Son Jesus Christ,
your living Word through whom you have
created all things;

Who was sent by you, in your great
goodness, to be our Saviour;
by the power of the Holy Spirit he took flesh
and, as your Son, born of the blessed Virgin,
was seen on earth
and went about among us;

He opened wide his arms for us on the
cross;
he put an end to death by dying for us
and revealed the resurrection by rising to
new life;
so he fulfilled your will and won for you a
holy people.

PROPER PREFACE, when appropriate (section 76)

Therefore with angels and archangels,
and with all the company of heaven,
we proclaim your great and glorious name,
for ever praising you and saying:

All   **Holy, holy, holy Lord,
God of power and might,
heaven and earth are full of your glory.
Hosanna in the highest.**

     [ASB/136]

This ANTHEM may also be used.

> **Blessed is he who comes in the name of**
> **the Lord.**
> **Hosanna in the highest.**

President   Lord, you are holy indeed, the source of
all holiness;
grant that, by the power of your Holy Spirit,
and according to your holy will,
these your gifts of bread and wine
may be to us the body and blood of our Lord
Jesus Christ;

Who in the same night that he was
betrayed,
took bread and gave you thanks;
he broke it and gave it to his disciples,
saying,
Take, eat; this is my body which is given
for you;
do this in remembrance of me.
In the same way, after supper
he took the cup and gave you thanks;
he gave it to them, saying,
Drink this, all of you;
this is my blood of the new covenant,
which is shed for you and for many for the
forgiveness of sins.
Do this, as often as you drink it,
in remembrance of me.

All   **Christ has died:**
Christ is risen:
Christ will come again.

President   And so, Father, calling to mind his death on
the cross,
his perfect sacrifice made once for the sins
of all men,

[ASB/137]

rejoicing at his mighty resurrection and
glorious ascension,
and looking for his coming in glory,
we celebrate this memorial of our
redemption;

We thank you for counting us worthy
to stand in your presence and serve you;
we bring before you this bread and this cup;

We pray you to accept this our duty
and service,
a spiritual sacrifice of praise and
thanksgiving;

Send the Holy Spirit on your people
and gather into one in your kingdom
all who share this one bread and one cup,
so that we, in the company of all the saints,
may praise and glorify you for ever,
through him from whom all good things
come,
Jesus Christ our Lord;

By whom, and with whom, and in whom,
in the unity of the Holy Spirit,
all honour and glory be yours, almighty
Father,
for ever and ever. **Amen.**

Silence may be kept.

*The service continues with THE LORD'S PRAYER at
section 42 on page 96.*

▶41.   *FOURTH EUCHARISTIC PRAYER*

President   The Lord be with you *or* The Lord is here.
All   **and also with you.   His Spirit is with us.**

President   Lift up your hearts.
All   **We lift them to the Lord.**

President   Let us give thanks to the Lord our God.
All   **It is right to give him thanks and praise.**

President   It is indeed right,
                 it is our duty and our joy,
                 at all times and in all places
                 to give you thanks and praise,
                 holy Father, heavenly King,
                 almighty and eternal God,
                 creator of heaven and earth,
                 through Jesus Christ our Lord:

PROPER PREFACE, when appropriate (section 76).
The following is used when no Proper Preface is
provided.

                 For he is the true high priest,
                 who has loosed us from our sins
                 and has made us to be a royal priesthood
                    to you,
                 our God and Father.

                 Therefore with angels and archangels,
                 and with all the company of heaven,
                 we proclaim your great and glorious name,
                 for ever praising you and saying:

All   **Holy, holy, holy Lord,**
                 God of power and might,
                 heaven and earth are full of your glory.
                 Hosanna in the highest.

This ANTHEM may also be used.

**Blessed is he who comes in the name of
the Lord.
Hosanna in the highest.**

President   All glory to you, our heavenly Father:
in your tender mercy
you gave your only Son Jesus Christ
to suffer death upon the cross for
    our redemption;
he made there
a full atonement for the sins of the
    whole world,
offering once for all his one sacrifice
    of himself;
he instituted,
and in his holy gospel commanded us
    to continue,
a perpetual memory of his precious death
until he comes again.

Hear us, merciful Father, we humbly pray,
and grant that by the power of your
    Holy Spirit
we who receive these gifts of your creation,
this bread and this wine,
according to your Son our Saviour Jesus
    Christ's holy institution,
in remembrance of the death that he
    suffered,
may be partakers of his most blessed body
    and blood;

Who in the same night that he was
    betrayed,
took bread and gave you thanks;
he broke it and gave it to his disciples,
    saying,

94   [ASB/140]

Take, eat; this is my body which is given
for you;
do this in remembrance of me.
In the same way, after supper
he took the cup and gave you thanks;
he gave it to them, saying,
Drink this, all of you;
this is my blood of the new covenant,
which is shed for you and for many for the
forgiveness of sins.
Do this, as often as you drink it,
in remembrance of me.

All   **Christ has died:**
Christ is risen:
Christ will come again.

President   Therefore, Lord and heavenly Father,
in remembrance of the precious death
and passion,
the mighty resurrection and glorious
ascension
of your dear Son Jesus Christ,
we offer you through him this sacrifice of
praise and thanksgiving.

Grant that by his merits and death,
and through faith in his blood,
we and all your Church may receive
forgiveness of our sins
and all other benefits of his passion.
Although we are unworthy, through our
many sins,
to offer you any sacrifice,
yet we pray that you will accept this,
the duty and service that we owe;
do not weigh our merits, but pardon
our offences,

[ASB/141]   95

and fill us all who share in this
   holy communion
with your grace and heavenly blessing.

Through Jesus Christ our Lord,
by whom, and with whom, and in whom,
in the unity of the Holy Spirit,
all honour and glory be yours, almighty
   Father,
now and for ever. **Amen.**

Silence may be kept.

THE COMMUNION

*THE BREAKING OF THE BREAD AND
THE GIVING OF THE BREAD AND CUP*

▶42. *THE LORD'S PRAYER is said either as follows or in its
traditional form.*

President As our Saviour taught us, so we pray.
All   **Our Father in heaven,
           hallowed be your name,
           your kingdom come,
           your will be done,
           on earth as in heaven.
           Give us today our daily bread.
           Forgive us our sins
           as we forgive those who sin against us.
           Lead us not into temptation
           but deliver us from evil.**

           **For the kingdom, the power, and the glory
              are yours
           now and for ever. Amen.**

▶43. *The president breaks the consecrated bread, saying*

           We break this bread
           to share in the body of Christ.

All   **Though we are many, we are one body, because we all share in one bread.**

44. *Either here or during the distribution one of the following anthems may be said.*

> **Lamb of God, you take away the sins of the world:**
> **have mercy on us.**
>
> **Lamb of God, you take away the sins of the world:**
> **have mercy on us.**
>
> **Lamb of God, you take away the sins of the world:**
> **grant us peace.**

or   **Jesus, Lamb of God: have mercy on us.**
Jesus, bearer of our sins: have mercy on us.
Jesus, redeemer of the world: give us
    your peace.

▶45. *Before the distribution the president says*

> Draw near with faith. Receive the body of our Lord Jesus Christ which he gave for you, and his blood which he shed for you.
>
> Eat and drink in remembrance that he died for you, and feed on him in your hearts by faith with thanksgiving.

Additional words of invitation may be used (see section 85).

▶46. *The president and people receive the communion. At the distribution the minister says to each communicant*

> The body of Christ keep you in eternal life.
> The blood of Christ keep you in eternal life.

or   The body of Christ.
The blood of Christ.

The communicant replies each time **Amen,** *and then receives. Alternative words of distribution may be found in section 66.*

47. *During the distribution HYMNS and ANTHEMS may be sung.*

▶48. *If either or both of the consecrated elements be likely to prove insufficient, the president himself returns to the holy table and adds more, saying these words.*

> Father, giving thanks over the bread and the cup according to the institution of your Son Jesus Christ, who said, Take, eat; this is my body (and/or Drink this; this is my blood), we pray that this bread/wine also may be to us his body/blood, to be received in remembrance of him.

49. *Any consecrated bread and wine which is not required for purposes of communion is consumed at the end of the distribution or after the service.*

AFTER COMMUNION

50. *AN APPROPRIATE SENTENCE may be said and A HYMN may be sung.*

▶51. *Either or both of the following prayers or other suitable prayers are said (see section 86).*

52. President Father of all, we give you thanks and praise, that when we were still far off you met us in your Son and brought us home. Dying and living, he declared your love, gave us grace, and opened the gate of glory. May we who share Christ's body live his risen life; we who drink his cup bring life to others; we whom the Spirit lights give light to the world. Keep us firm in the hope you have set before us, so we and all your children

shall be free, and the whole earth live to
praise your name; through Christ our Lord.
Amen.

or

53. **All**   **Almighty God,**
we thank you for feeding us
with the body and blood of your Son
    Jesus Christ.
Through him we offer you our souls and
    bodies
to be a living sacrifice.
Send us out
in the power of your Spirit
to live and work
to your praise and glory. Amen.

THE DISMISSAL

54. *The president may say this or an alternative BLESSING*
(section 77).

The peace of God, which passes all
understanding, keep your hearts and
minds in the knowledge and love of God,
and of his Son Jesus Christ our Lord; and
the blessing of God almighty, the Father,
the Son, and the Holy Spirit, be among you,
and remain with you always. **Amen.**

▶55. President   Go in peace to love and serve the Lord.
    All   **In the name of Christ. Amen.**

or

    President   Go in the peace of Christ.
    All   **Thanks be to God.**

From Easter Day to Pentecost 'Alleluia! Alleluia!' may
be added after both the versicle and the response.

▶56. *The ministers and people depart.*

THE ORDER FOLLOWING THE PATTERN OF THE BOOK OF COMMON PRAYER

(continued from section 22)

▶ 57. *The priest prepares the bread and wine on the holy table, the offerings of the people may be presented, and A HYMN may be sung.*

58. *THE COMMANDMENTS (section 78) or the following SUMMARY OF THE LAW may be said.*

Minister Our Lord Jesus Christ said: The first commandment is this: 'Hear, O Israel, the Lord our God is the only Lord. You shall love the Lord your God with all your heart, with all your soul, with all your mind, and with all your strength.'
The second is this: 'Love your neighbour as yourself.' There is no other commandment greater than these.

All **Amen. Lord, have mercy.**

▶ 59. *The priest invites the congregation to confess their sins in these or other suitable words (see section 25). Alternative confessions may be used (see section 80).*

Let us confess our sins, in penitence and faith, firmly resolved to keep God's commandments and to live in love and peace with all men.

▶ 60. **All** **Almighty God, our heavenly Father,
we have sinned against you and against
  our fellow men,
in thought and word and deed,
through negligence, through weakness,
through our own deliberate fault.
We are truly sorry,
and repent of all our sins.
For the sake of your Son Jesus Christ, who
  died for us,**

forgive us all that is past;
and grant that we may serve you in
　　newness of life
to the glory of your name. Amen

▶61. Priest　　　Almighty God,
who forgives all who truly repent,
have mercy upon you,
pardon and deliver you from all your sins,
confirm and strengthen you in all
　　goodness,
and keep you in life eternal;
through Jesus Christ our Lord. **Amen.**

▶62. *The priest says these SENTENCES.*

Hear the words of comfort our Saviour
Christ says to all who truly turn to him:
Come to me, all who labour and are heavy
laden, and I will give you rest.
　　　　　　　　　　　　Matthew 11.28

God so loved the world that he gave his
only Son, that whoever believes in him
should not perish but have eternal life.
　　　　　　　　　　　　John 3.16

Hear what Saint Paul says: This saying is
true and worthy of full acceptance, that
Christ Jesus came into the world to save
sinners.　　　　　　　*Timothy 1.15*

Hear what Saint John says: If anyone sins,
we have an advocate with the Father, Jesus
Christ the righteous; and he is the
propitiation for our sins.　　　*1 John 2.1*

▶63. Priest　　　Lift up your hearts.
　　　All　　　**We lift them to the Lord.**

　　　Priest　　　Let us give thanks to the Lord our God.
　　　All　　　**It is right to give him thanks and praise.**

Priest   It is indeed right,
it is our duty and our joy,
at all times and in all places
to give you thanks and praise,
holy Father, heavenly King,
almighty and eternal God,
through Jesus Christ our Lord.

PROPER PREFACE, when appropriate (section 76)

         Therefore with angels and archangels,
and with all the company of heaven,
we proclaim your great and glorious name,
for ever praising you and saying:

All   **Holy, holy, holy Lord,
God of power and might,
heaven and earth are full of your glory.
Hosanna in the highest.**

▶64. **All**   **We do not presume
to come to this your table, merciful Lord,
trusting in our own righteousness,
but in your manifold and great mercies.
We are not worthy
so much as to gather up the crumbs under
    your table.
But you are the same Lord
whose nature is always to have mercy.
Grant us therefore, gracious Lord,
so to eat the flesh of your dear Son
    Jesus Christ
and to drink his blood,
that we may evermore dwell in him
and he in us. Amen.**

▶65. Priest   Almighty God, our heavenly Father,
in your tender mercy
you gave your only Son Jesus Christ
to suffer death upon the cross for
    our redemption;

he made there
a full atonement for the sins of the
     whole world,
offering once for all his one sacrifice
     of himself;
he instituted,
and in his holy gospel commanded us
     to continue,
a perpetual memory of his precious death
until he comes again.

Hear us, merciful Father, we humbly pray,
and grant that we who receive these gifts of
     your creation,
this bread and this wine,
according to your Son our Saviour Jesus
     Christ's holy institution,
in remembrance of the death that he
     suffered,
may be partakers of his most blessed body
     and blood;

Who in the same night that he was
     betrayed,
Here the priest takes the paten.
took bread and gave you thanks;
he broke it, *Here he breaks the bread.*
and gave it to his disciples, saying,
Take, eat;
Here he lays his hand on all the bread.
this is my body which is given for you;
do this in remembrance of me.
In the same way, after supper
Here he takes the cup.
he took the cup and gave you thanks;
he gave it to them, saying,
Drink this, all of you;
*Here he lays his hand on all the vessels of
wine to be consecrated.*
this is my blood of the new covenant,

which is shed for you and for many for the
forgiveness of sins.
Do this, as often as you drink it,
in remembrance of me. **Amen.**

▶66. *The priest and people receive the communion. At the
distribution the minister says to the communicants the
following words, or those in sections 45 and 46.*

The body of our Lord Jesus Christ, which
was given for you, preserve your body and
soul to eternal life. Take and eat this in
remembrance that Christ died for you, and
feed on him in your heart by faith with
thanksgiving.

The blood of our Lord Jesus Christ, which
was shed for you, preserve your body and
soul to eternal life. Drink this in remembrance that Christ's blood was shed for you,
and be thankful.

▶67. *If either or both of the consecrated elements be likely to
prove insufficient, the priest himself returns to the holy
table and adds more, and consecrates according to the
form in section 65, beginning, 'Our Saviour Christ in
the same night...,' for the bread, and at 'In the same
way, after supper our Saviour...,' for the cup.*

▶68. *Any consecrated bread and wine which is not required
for purposes of communion is consumed at the end of
the distribution or after the service.*

▶69. *THE LORD'S PRAYER is said either as follows or in its
traditional form.*

Priest   As our Saviour taught us, so we pray.
All   **Our Father in heaven,**
          hallowed be your name,
          your kingdom come,
          your will be done,
          on earth as in heaven.

Give us today our daily bread.
Forgive us our sins
as we forgive those who sin against us.
Lead us not into temptation
but deliver us from evil.

For the kingdom, the power, and the glory
  are yours
now and for ever. Amen.

70. *One or other of the following prayers or one of those at sections 52 and 53 is used.*

71.

Lord and heavenly Father, we your servants entirely desire your fatherly goodness mercifully to accept this our sacrifice of praise and thanksgiving, and to grant that, by the merits and death of your Son Jesus Christ, and through faith in his blood, we and your whole Church may receive forgiveness of our sins and all other benefits of his passion.

And here we offer and present to you, O Lord, ourselves, our souls and bodies, to be a reasonable, holy, and living sacrifice, humbly beseeching you that all we who are partakers of this holy communion may be fulfilled with your grace and heavenly benediction.

And although we are unworthy, through our many sins, to offer you any sacrifice, yet we pray that you will accept this, the duty and service that we owe, not weighing our merits but pardoning our offences, through Jesus Christ our Lord; by whom and with whom, in the unity of the Holy Spirit, all honour and glory are yours, Father almighty, now and for ever. **Amen.**

or

72.   Almighty and everlasting God, we heartily
thank you that you graciously feed us, who
have duly received these holy mysteries,
with the spiritual food of the most precious
body and blood of your Son our Saviour
Jesus Christ, and assure us thereby of your
favour and goodness towards us and that
we are true members of the mystical body
of your Son, the blessed company of all
faithful people, and are also heirs, through
hope, of your eternal kingdom, by the
merits of the most precious death and
passion of your dear Son. And we humbly
beseech you, heavenly Father, so to assist
us with your grace, that we may continue in
that holy fellowship, and do all such good
works as you have prepared for us to walk
in; through Jesus Christ our Lord, to whom,
with you and the Holy Spirit, be all honour
and glory, now and for ever. **Amen.**

73.   *GLORIA IN EXCELSIS or A HYMN may be sung.*

All   **Glory to God in the highest,**
and peace to his people on earth.

Lord God, heavenly King,
almighty God and Father,
we worship you, we give you thanks,
we praise you for your glory.

Lord Jesus Christ, only Son of the Father,
Lord God, Lamb of God,
you take away the sin of the world:
have mercy on us;
you are seated at the right hand of the
    Father:
receive our prayer.

For you alone are the Holy One,
you alone are the Lord,
you alone are the Most High,
Jesus Christ,
with the Holy Spirit,
in the glory of God the Father, Amen.

74. Priest   The peace of God, which passes all understanding, keep your hearts and minds in the knowledge and love of God, and of his Son Jesus Christ our Lord; and the blessing of God almighty, the Father, the Son, and the Holy Spirit, be among you, and remain with you always. **Amen.**

75. *The ministers and people depart.*

APPENDICES

76. PROPER PREFACES

Suitable for use with all Eucharistic Prayers (sections 38, 39, 40, and 41) and the Order following the pattern of the Book of Common Prayer (section 63).

Advent
1. And now we give you thanks because in his coming as man the day of our deliverance has dawned; and through him you will make all things new, as he comes in power and triumph to judge the world.

2. And now we give you thanks because you prepared the way of your Son Jesus Christ by the preaching of your servant John the Baptist, who proclaimed him as the Lamb of God, our Saviour.

The Incarnation
3. And now we give you thanks because by the power of the Holy Spirit he took our nature upon him and was born of the Virgin Mary his mother, that being himself without sin he might make us clean from all sin.

4. And now we give you thanks because in the incarnation of the Word a new light has dawned upon the world; you have become one with us that we might become one with you in your glorious kingdom.

5. And now we give you thanks because in coming to dwell among us as man, he revealed the radiance of your glory, and brought us out of darkness into your own marvellous light.

6. And now we give you thanks because in choosing the blessed Virgin Mary to be the mother of your Son you have exalted the humble and meek. Your angel hailed her as most highly favoured; with all generations we call her blessed, and with her we rejoice and magnify your holy name.

7. And now we give you thanks because in his earthly childhood you entrusted him to the care of a human family. In Mary and Joseph you give us an example of love and devotion to him, and also a pattern of family life.

Lent
8. And now we give you thanks because through him you have given us the spirit of discipline, that we may triumph over evil and grow in grace.

The Cross
9. And now we give you thanks because for our sins he was lifted high upon the cross that he might draw the whole world to himself; and, by his suffering and death, became the source of eternal salvation for all who put their trust in him.

10. And now we give you thanks because for our salvation he was obedient even to death on the cross. The tree of shame was made the tree of glory; and where life was lost, there life has been restored.

Maundy Thursday
11. And now we give you thanks because when his hour had come, in his great love he gave this supper to his disciples, that we might proclaim his death, and feast with him in his kingdom.

The Blessing of the Oils
12. And now we give you thanks because by your Holy Spirit you anointed your only Son to be servant of all and ordained that he should enter into his kingdom through suffering. In your wisdom and love you call your Church to serve the world, to share in Christ's suffering and to reveal his glory.

The Resurrection
13. And now we give you thanks because you raised him gloriously from the dead. For he is the true Paschal Lamb who was offered for us and has taken away the sin of the world. By his death he has destroyed death, and by his rising again he has restored to us eternal life.

14.   And now we give you thanks because in his victory over the grave a new age has dawned, the long reign of sin is ended, a broken world is being renewed, and man is once again made whole.

15.   And now we give you thanks because through him you have given us eternal life, and delivered us from the bondage of sin and the fear of death into the glorious liberty of the children of God.

16.   And now we give you thanks because through him you have given us the hope of a glorious resurrection; so that, although death comes to us all, yet we rejoice in the promise of eternal life; for to your faithful people life is changed, not taken away; and when our mortal flesh is laid aside, an everlasting dwelling place is made ready for us in heaven.

The Ascension
17.   And now we give you thanks because you have highly exalted him, and given him the name which is above all other names, that at the name of Jesus every knee shall bow.

Pentecost: Baptism and Confirmation
18.   And now we give you thanks because by the Holy Spirit you lead us into all truth, and give us power to proclaim your gospel to the nations, and to serve you as a royal priesthood.

Trinity Sunday
19.   And now we give you thanks because you have revealed your glory as the glory of your Son and of the Holy Spirit: three persons equal in majesty, undivided in splendour, yet one Lord, one God, ever to be worshipped and adored.

The Transfiguration
20.   And now we give you thanks because the divine glory of the incarnate Word shone forth upon the holy mountain; and your own voice from heaven proclaimed your beloved Son.

St Michael and All Angels
21.   Through him the archangels sing your praise, the angels fulfil your commands, the cherubim and seraphim continually proclaim your holiness; the whole company of heaven glorifies your name and rejoices to do your will. Therefore we pray that our voices may be heard with theirs, for ever praising you and saying:

All   **Holy, holy, holy Lord...**

All Saints' Day
22.   And now we give you thanks for the hope to which you call us in your Son, that following in the faith of all your saints, we may run with perseverance the race that is set before us, and with them receive the unfading crown of glory.

Apostles and Evangelists
23.   And now we give you thanks because your Son Jesus Christ after his resurrection sent forth his apostles and evangelists to preach the gospel to all nations and to teach us the way of truth.

Martyrs
24.   And now we give you thanks that in the witness of your martyrs who followed Christ even to death you revealed your power made perfect in our human weakness.

Saints' Days
25.   And now we give you thanks for the work of your grace in the life of Saint N and that by the same grace you lead us in the way of holiness setting before us the vision of your glory.

Dedication
26.   And now we give you thanks for your blessing on this house of prayer, where through your grace we offer you the sacrifice of praise, and are built by your Spirit into a temple made without hands, even the body of your Son Jesus Christ.

Marriage
27.   And now we give you thanks because you have made the union between Christ and his Church a pattern for the marriage between husband and wife.

Ordination
28.   And now we give you thanks because within the royal priesthood of your Church you ordain ministers to proclaim the word of God, to care for your people and to celebrate the sacraments of the new covenant.

Unity
29.   And now we give you thanks because of the unity that you have given us in your Son and that you are the God and Father of us all, above all and through all and in all.

Baptism
30.   And now we give you thanks because through baptism we have been buried with Christ so that we may rise with him to the new life.

Suitable for use with the Fourth Eucharistic Prayer (section 41) and the Order following the pattern of the Book of Common Prayer (section 63).

Sundays
31.   And now we give you thanks because you are the source of light and life; you made us in your image, and called us to new life in him.

32.   And now we give you thanks because on the first day of the week he overcame death and the grave and opened to us the way of everlasting life.

33.   And now we give you thanks because by water and the Holy Spirit you have made us in him a new people to show forth your glory.

77. ALTERNATIVE BLESSINGS

Advent
Christ the Sun of Righteousness shine upon you and scatter the darkness from before your path; and the blessing...

Christmas
Christ, who by his incarnation gathered into one all things earthly and heavenly, fill you with his joy and peace; and the blessing...

or

Christ the Son of God, born of Mary, fill you with his grace to trust his promises and obey his will; and the blessing...

Epiphany
Christ the Son of God gladden your hearts with the good news of his kingdom; and the blessing...

Ash Wednesday to Lent 4
Christ give you grace to grow in holiness, to deny yourselves, take up your cross, and follow him; and the blessing...

Lent 5 and Holy Week
Christ crucified draw you to himself, to find in him a sure ground for faith, a firm support for hope, and the assurance of sins forgiven; and the blessing...

Easter
The God of peace, who brought again from the dead our Lord Jesus, that great shepherd of the sheep, through the blood of the eternal covenant, make you perfect in every good work to do his will, working in you that which is well-pleasing in his sight; and the blessing...

or

The God of peace, who brought again from the dead our Lord Jesus, that great shepherd of the sheep, make you perfect in every good work to do his will; and the blessing...

or

God the Father, by whose glory Christ was raised from the dead, strengthen you to walk with him in his risen life; and the blessing...

or

God, who through the resurrection of our Lord Jesus Christ has given us the victory, give you joy and peace in your faith; and the blessing...

Ascension
Christ our king make you faithful and strong to do his will, that you may reign with him in glory; and the blessing...

Pentecost
The Spirit of truth lead you into all truth, give you grace to confess that Jesus Christ is Lord, and to proclaim the word and works of God; and the blessing...

Trinity Sunday
God the Holy Trinity make you strong in faith and love, defend you on every side, and guide you in truth and peace; and the blessing...

Saints' Days
God give you grace to follow his saints in faith and hope and love; and the blessing...

or

God give you grace to follow his saints in faith and truth and gentleness; and the blessing...

or

God give you grace to share the inheritance of his saints in glory; and the blessing...

Unity
Christ the Good Shepherd, who laid down his life for the sheep, draw you and all who hear his voice to be one within one fold; and the blessing...

General
The God of all grace who called you to his eternal glory in Christ Jesus, establish, strengthen and settle you in the faith; and the blessing...

or
God, who from the death of sin raised you to new life in Christ, keep you from falling and set you in the presence of his glory; and the blessing...

or

Christ who has nourished us with himself the living bread, make you one in praise and love, and raise you up at the last day; and the blessing...

or

The God of peace fill you with all joy and hope in believing; and the blessing...

78. THE COMMANDMENTS

Either A:

Minister   Our Lord Jesus Christ said, If you love me, keep my commandments; happy are those who hear the word of God and keep it. Hear then these commandments which God has given to his people, and take them to heart.

              I am the Lord your God: you shall have no other gods but me.
              You shall love the Lord your God with all your heart, with all your soul, with all your mind and with all your strength.

All   **Amen. Lord, have mercy.**

Minister	You shall not make for yourself any idol.
	God is spirit, and those who worship him must worship in spirit and in truth.
All	**Amen. Lord, have mercy.**

Minister	You shall not dishonour the name of the Lord your God.
	You shall worship him with awe and reverence.
All	**Amen. Lord, have mercy.**

Minister	Remember the Lord's day and keep it holy.
	Christ is risen from the dead: set your minds on things that are above, not on things that are on the earth.
All	**Amen. Lord, have mercy.**

Minister	Honour your father and mother.
	Live as servants of God; honour all men; love the brotherhood.
All	**Amen. Lord, have mercy.**

Minister	You shall not commit murder.
	Be reconciled to your brother; overcome evil with good.
All	**Amen. Lord, have mercy.**

Minister	You shall not commit adultery.
	Know that your body is a temple of the Holy Spirit.
All	**Amen. Lord, have mercy.**

Minister	You shall not steal.
	Be honest in all that you do and care for those in need.
All	**Amen. Lord, have mercy.**

Minister	You shall not be a false witness.
	Let everyone speak the truth.
All	**Amen. Lord, have mercy.**

[ASB/162]

Minister	You shall not covet anything which belongs to your neighbour.
	Remember the words of the Lord Jesus: It is more blessed to give than to receive. Love your neighbour as yourself, for love is the fulfilling of the law.
All	**Amen. Lord, have mercy.**

or B:

Minister	God spoke all these words, saying, I am the Lord your God (who brought you out of the land of Egypt, out of the house of bondage). You shall have no other gods before me.
All	**Amen. Lord, have mercy.**

Minister	You shall not make for yourself a graven image (or any likeness of anything that is in heaven above, or that is in the earth beneath, or that is in the water under the earth; you shall not bow down to them or serve them; for I the Lord your God am a jealous God, visiting the iniquity of the fathers upon the children to the third and the fourth generation of those who hate me, but showing steadfast love to thousands of those who love me and keep my commandments).
All	**Amen. Lord, have mercy.**

Minister	You shall not take the name of the Lord your God in vain (for the Lord will not hold him guiltless who takes his name in vain).
All	**Amen. Lord, have mercy.**

Minister	Remember the sabbath day, to keep it holy. (Six days you shall labour, and do all your work; but the seventh day is a sabbath to the Lord your God; in it you shall not do any work, you, or your son, or your daughter, your manservant, or your maidservant, or your cattle, or the sojourner who

	is within your gates; for in six days the Lord made heaven and earth, the sea, and all that is in them, and rested the seventh day; therefore the Lord blessed the sabbath day and hallowed it.)
All	**Amen. Lord, have mercy.**

Minister	Honour your father and your mother (that your days may be long in the land which the Lord your God gives you).
All	**Amen. Lord, have mercy.**

Minister	You shall not kill.
All	**Amen. Lord, have mercy.**

Minister	You shall not commit adultery.
All	**Amen. Lord, have mercy.**

Minister	You shall not steal.
All	**Amen. Lord, have mercy.**

Minister	You shall not bear false witness against your neighbour.
All	**Amen. Lord, have mercy.**

Minister	You shall not covet (your neighbour's house; you shall not covet your neighbour's wife, or his manservant, or his maidservant, or his ox, or his ass, or) anything that is your neighbour's.
All	**Lord, have mercy on us, and write all these your laws in our hearts.**

79. KYRIE ELEISON

Section 9 may be said in one of the following forms.

Lord, have mercy (upon us.)	Kyrie eleison.
Lord, have mercy (upon us.)	**Kyrie eleison.**
Lord, have mercy (upon us.)	Kyrie eleison.

Christ, have mercy (upon us.)	**Christe eleison.**
Christ, have mercy (upon us.)	Christe eleison.
Christ, have mercy (upon us.)	**Christe eleison.**
Lord, have mercy (upon us.)	Kyrie eleison.
Lord, have mercy (upon us.)	**Kyrie eleison.**
Lord, have mercy (upon us.)	Kyrie eleison.

80. ALTERNATIVE CONFESSIONS

Either A:

All   Almighty God, our heavenly Father,
we have sinned against you and against
   our fellow men,
in thought and word and deed,
in the evil we have done
and in the good we have not done,
through ignorance, through weakness,
through our own deliberate fault.
We are truly sorry,
and repent of all our sins.
For the sake of your Son Jesus Christ, who
   died for us,
forgive us all that is past;
and grant that we may serve you in
   newness of life
to the glory of your name. Amen.

or B:

All   Almighty God, our heavenly Father,
we have sinned against you,
through our own fault,
in thought and word and deed,
and in what we have left undone.
For your Son our Lord Jesus Christ's sake,
forgive us all that is past;
and grant that we may serve you in
   newness of life
to the glory of your name. Amen.

or C:

All   Father eternal, giver of light and grace,
we have sinned against you and against
    our fellow men,
in what we have thought,
in what we have said and done,
through ignorance, through weakness,
through our own deliberate fault.
We have wounded your love,
and marred your image in us.
We are sorry and ashamed,
and repent of all our sins.
For the sake of your Son Jesus Christ, who
    died for us,
forgive us all that is past;
and lead us out from darkness
to walk as children of light. Amen.

81.   *ALTERNATIVE FORMS OF INTERCESSION*

Either A:

Minister   Let us pray for the whole Church of God in Christ
Jesus, and for all men according to their needs.

O God, the creator and preserver of all mankind,
we pray for men of every race, and in every kind
of need: make your ways known on earth, your
saving power among all nations. (Especially we
pray for...)
Lord, in your mercy

All   **hear our prayer**

Minister	We pray for your Church throughout the world: guide and govern us by your Holy Spirit, that all who profess and call themselves Christians may be led into the way of truth, and hold the faith in unity of spirit, in the bond of peace, and in righteousness of life. (Especially we pray for...) Lord, in your mercy
All	**hear our prayer.**

Minister	We commend to your fatherly goodness all who are anxious or distressed in mind or body; comfort and relieve them in their need; give them patience in their sufferings, and bring good out of their troubles. (Especially we pray for...) Merciful Father,
All	**accept these prayers for the sake of your Son, our Saviour Jesus Christ. Amen.**

or B:

Minister	In the power of the Spirit and in union with Christ, let us pray to the Father.
	Hear our prayers, O Lord our God.
All	**Hear us, good Lord.**

Minister	Govern and direct your holy Church; fill it with love and truth; and grant it that unity which is your will.
All	**Hear us, good Lord.**

Minister	Give us boldness to preach the gospel in all the world, and to make disciples of all the nations.
All	**Hear us, good Lord.**

Minister	Enlighten your ministers with knowledge and understanding, that by their teaching and their lives they may proclaim your word.
All	**Hear us, good Lord.**

[ASB/167]

Minister	Give your people grace to hear and receive your word, and to bring forth the fruit of the Spirit.
All	**Hear us, good Lord.**
Minister	Bring into the way of truth all who have erred and are deceived.
All	**Hear us, good Lord.**
Minister	Strengthen those who stand; comfort and help the faint-hearted; raise up the fallen; and finally beat down Satan under our feet.
All	**Hear us, good Lord.**
Minister	Guide the leaders of the nations into the ways of peace and justice.
All	**Hear us, good Lord.**
Minister	Guard and strengthen your servant Elizabeth our Queen, that she may put her trust in you, and seek your honour and glory.
All	**Hear us, good Lord.**
Minister	Endue the High Court of Parliament and all the Ministers of the Crown with wisdom and understanding.
All	**Hear us, good Lord.**
Minister	Bless those who administer the law, that they may uphold justice, honesty, and truth.
All	**Hear us, good Lord.**
Minister	Teach us to use the fruits of the earth to your glory, and for the good of all mankind.
All	**Hear us, good Lord.**
Minister	Bless and keep all your people.
All	**Hear us, good Lord.**
Minister	Help and comfort the lonely, the bereaved, and the oppressed.
All	**Lord, have mercy.**

Minister	Keep in safety those who travel, and all who are in danger.
All	**Lord, have mercy.**
Minister	Heal the sick in body and mind, and provide for the homeless, the hungry, and the destitute.
All	**Lord, have mercy.**
Minister	Show your pity on prisoners and refugees, and all who are in trouble.
All	**Lord, have mercy.**
Minister	Forgive our enemies, persecutors, and slanderers, and turn their hearts.
All	**Lord, have mercy.**
Minister	Hear us as we remember those who have died in the peace of Christ, both those who have confessed the faith and those whose faith is known to you alone, and grant us with them a share in your eternal kingdom.
All	**Lord, have mercy.**
Minister	Father, you hear those who pray in the name of your Son: grant that what we have asked in faith we may obtain according to your will; through Jesus Christ our Lord. **Amen.**

82. *ALTERNATIVE PRAYER OF HUMBLE ACCESS*
   (section 29)

> **Most merciful Lord,**
> **your love compels us to come in.**
> **Our hands were unclean,**
> **our hearts were unprepared;**
> **we were not fit**
> **even to eat the crumbs from under your table.**
> **But you, Lord, are the God of our salvation,**
> **and share your bread with sinners.**
> **So cleanse and feed us**
> **with the precious body and blood of your Son,**
> **that he may live in us and we in him;**
> **and that we, with the whole company of Christ,**
> **may sit and eat in your kingdom. Amen.**

83. *A SELECTION OF OTHER INTRODUCTORY WORDS*
   TO THE PEACE (section 30)

Advent, Christmas, Epiphany
Our Saviour Christ is the Prince of Peace; of the increase of his government and of peace there shall be no end.

Lent
Being justified by faith, we have peace with God through our Lord Jesus Christ.

Easter, Ascension
The risen Christ came and stood among his disciples and said, Peace be with you. Then they were glad when they saw the Lord.

Pentecost
The fruit of the Spirit is love, joy, peace. If we live in the Spirit, let us walk in the Spirit.

Saints' Days
We are fellow-citizens with the saints, and of the household of God, through Christ our Lord who came and preached peace to those who were far off and those who were near.

85. *ADDITIONAL WORDS OF INVITATION TO COMMUNION which may be used after section 45*

Either A:

President   Jesus is the Lamb of God
who takes away the sins of the world.
Happy are those who are called to his supper.

All   **Lord, I am not worthy to receive you,
but only say the word, and I shall be healed.**

or B:

President   The gifts of God for the people of God.
All   **Jesus Christ is holy,
Jesus Christ is Lord,
to the glory of God the Father.**

or C: Easter Day to Pentecost

President: Alleluia! Christ our Passover is sacrificed
for us.
All   **Alleluia! Let us keep the feast.**

86. *ALTERNATIVE FINAL PRAYER*

Especially suitable for a service without Communion

All   **Almighty God,
we offer you our souls and bodies,
to be a living sacrifice,
through Jesus Christ our Lord.
Send us out into the world
in the power of your Spirit,
to live and work
to your praise and glory. Amen.**

NOTES

1. *Preparation*   Careful devotional preparation before the service is recommended for every communicant.

2. *The President*   The president (who, in accordance with the provisions of Canon B12 'Of the ministry of the Holy Communion', must have been episcopally ordained priest) presides over the whole service. He says the opening Greeting, the Collect, the Absolution, the Peace, and the Blessing; he himself must take the bread and the cup before replacing them on the holy table, say the Eucharistic Prayer, break the consecrated bread, and receive the sacrament on every occasion. The remaining parts of the service he may delegate to others. When necessity dictates, a deacon or lay person may preside over the Ministry of the Word.

When the Bishop is present, it is appropriate that he should act as president. He may also delegate sections 32-49 to a priest.

3. *Posture*   When a certain posture is particularly appropriate, it is indicated after the section number. For the rest of the service local custom may be established and followed. The Eucharistic Prayer (sections 38, 39, 40, and 41) is a single prayer, the unity of which may be obscured by changes of posture in the course of it.

4. *Seasonal Material*   The seasonal sentences and blessings are optional. Any other appropriate scriptural sentences may be read at sections 1 and 50 at the discretion of the president and 'Alleluia' may be added to any sentence from Easter Day until Pentecost.

5. *Greetings (section 2 etc.)*   In addition to the points where greetings are provided, at other suitable points (e.g. before the Gospel and before the Blessing and Dismissal) the minister may say 'The Lord be with you' and the congregation reply 'and also with you'.

6. *Prayers of Penitence*   These are used after either section 4 or section 23 (but see Note 22 below for occasions when the Order following the pattern of the Book of Common Prayer is used).

7. *Kyrie eleison (section 9)*   This may be used in English or Greek. Alternative versions are set out in section 79.

8. *Gloria in excelsis (sections 10 and 73)*   This canticle may be appropriately omitted during Advent and Lent, and on weekdays which are not Principal or Greater Holy Days. It may also be used at sections 1 and 16.

9. *The Collect (section 11)*   The Collect may be introduced by the words 'Let us pray' and a brief bidding, after which silence may be kept.

10. *Readings*   Where one of the three readings is to be omitted, provision for this is found in Table 3 of the Alternative Calendar and Lectionary according to the season of the year.

11. *The Gospel in Holy Week (section 17)*   From Palm Sunday to the Wednesday in Holy Week, and on Good Friday, the Passion Gospel may be introduced: 'The Passion of our Lord Jesus Christ according to N', and concluded: 'This is the Passion of the Lord'. No responses are used.

12. *The Sermon (section 18)*   The sermon is an integral part of the Ministry of the Word. A sermon should normally be preached at all celebrations on Sundays and other Holy Days.

13. *Proper Prefaces*   The Proper Prefaces are set out in section 76. They are obligatory when this is indicated in the seasonal propers but may be used on other suitable occasions. The Sunday Prefaces (31), (32), and (33) are for use with the Fourth Eucharistic Prayer and the Order following the pattern of the Book of Common Prayer.

14. *Second Eucharistic Prayer (section 39)*   The three paragraphs beginning 'For he is your living Word' and

ending 'a people for your own possession' may be omitted if a Proper Preface is used.

15. *Acclamations* These are optional. They may be introduced by the president with the words 'Let us proclaim the mystery of faith' or with other suitable words or they may be used without introduction.

16. *Manual Acts* In addition to the taking of the bread and the cup at section 36 the president may use traditional manual acts during the Eucharistic Prayers.

17. *Words of Invitation (section 45)* The words provided are to be used at least on Sundays and other Holy Days, and those in section 85 may be added. On other days those in section 85 may be substituted.

18. *The Blessing (section 54)* In addition to the blessings provided here and in section 77 the president may at his discretion use others.

19. *Notices* Banns of marriage and other notices may be published after section 2, section 19, or section 53.

20. *Hymns, Canticles, the Peace, the Collection and Presentation of the Offerings of the People, and the Preparation of the Gifts of Bread and Wine* Points are indicated for these, but if occasion requires they may occur elsewhere.

21. *Silence* After sections 6, 13, 15, 17, 18, 26, before sections 42 and 51, and after the biddings in section 21, silence may be kept.

22. *The Order following the pattern of the Book of Common Prayer (sections 22 and 57-75)* When this Order is being followed the Prayers of Penitence should not be used at section 4, as they are requisite at section 59. The Order provided should then be followed in its entirety.